THE FUTURE OF WEAPONS OF MASS DESTRUCTION

AN UPDATE

John P. Caves, Jr. and W. Seth Carus

National Intelligence University
National Intelligence Press
Washington, DC

February 2021

ACKNOWLEDGMENTS

While the authors are solely responsible for the final content of this paper, they benefited greatly from the time, expertise and support freely availed to them by many knowledgeable individuals and organizations. They include Mr. Caves' colleagues at National Intelligence University (NIU), where he worked on this paper while on a detail assignment from National Defense University (NDU). Mr. Caves expresses particular gratitude to Dr. Brian Holmes, dean of the Anthony G. Oettinger School of Science and Technology Intelligence, for his leadership, knowledge, and support. Dr. Sharon Adams, Ms. Beverly Barnhart, Mr. George Clifford, Dr. LaMesha Craft, and Dr. R. Carter Morris offered helpful comments on the paper at various stages. They and Mr. Damarius Alston, LTC Jeffrey Bacon, Lt Col Frances Deutch, Ms. Thelma Flamer, Mr. Julian Meade, and Ms. Christina Sanders were among others at NIU whose assistance and support made Mr. Caves' assignment at NIU enjoyable as well as productive.

Both authors are deeply indebted to their colleagues at NDU's Center for the Study of Weapons of Mass Destruction (CSWMD), especially Mr. Brendan Melley, director of the CSWMD; Mr. Patrick Terrell, deputy director; Dr. Diane DiEuliis, assistant director; Dr. Justin Anderson; Dr. Samantha Arnett; Mr. Paul Bernstein; Dr. Gerald Epstein; Dr. Susan Koch; Ms. Amanda Moodie; and Dr. Shane Smith. They conducted the most comprehensive review of the draft manuscript, in some cases on multiple versions, and provided the most significant comments.

The authors also benefitted from the knowledge of experts at the Pacific Northwest National Laboratory and the Lawrence Livermore National Laboratory, and of Dr. Thomas Hammes from NDU's Center for Strategic Research, a sister organization to the CSWMD within the Institute for National Strategic Studies. They further appreciate the review and comments of John Caves III and Andrew Caves.

CONTENTS

EXECUTIVE SUMMARY

In 2014, the Center for the Study of Weapons of Mass Destruction at National Defense University published a paper on the future of weapons of mass destruction (WMD).[1] It projected WMD-relevant geopolitical and technological trends and made judgments as to how those trends would shape the nature and role of WMD in 2030. Significant geopolitical and technological developments bearing on the future of WMD have emerged since the 2014 paper or were largely not addressed in that study. This paper addresses six baskets of such developments. They include 1) the shifting roles of the great powers; 2) new pressures on arms control and nonproliferation regimes; 3) more roles for chemical and biological weapons; 4) expanding use of financial sanctions as an instrument of nonproliferation and other policies; 5) new types of delivery vehicles and more scope to develop and deploy them; and 6) other emerging and disruptive technologies with WMD relevance including artificial intelligence, biotechnology, quantum systems, and additive manufacturing. This paper was finalized in early November 2020 so does not address later events like the 2020 U.S. presidential election result.

The emergence of more capable and assertive great power rivals coupled with a United States that is more focused on its parochial interests than perhaps at any time since World War II can be expected to lead some other states, especially some U.S. allies and partners, to explore more earnestly alternatives to reliance upon U.S. leadership and protection to ensure their security in a more uncertain world. Nuclear weapons, and perhaps other forms of WMD, are among the alternatives available to them, and there is evidence that some are considering such options.

An apparent retreat from nuclear arms control, unraveling of the Joint Comprehensive Plan of Action (JCPOA), continued expansion and enhancement of nuclear arsenals in North Korea and South Asia, and recent extensive use of chemical weapons are reducing legal, normative, and practical barriers to WMD proliferation and use. The increasing and increasingly contentious wielding of U.S. financial clout through financial sanctions is sowing the seeds of its own demise, promising to diminish over time the utility of this powerful weapon against proliferation and other bad behavior.

The end of the Intermediate-Range Nuclear Forces (INF) Treaty and technological and engineering advances bearing on hypersonic and unmanned systems, remote sensing, and perhaps also nuclear propulsion are enabling development and deployment of ways to deliver nuclear and conventional payloads over longer distances with greater speed, maneuverability, and precision. These developments are blurring the lines between nuclear and conventional operations and between strategic and operational effects. Emerging or disruptive technologies, including artificial intelligence, biotechnology, quantum systems, and additive manufacturing, are expected to enhance these capabilities, enable the creation of new ones, and make some existing capabilities more accessible.

These developments pose more challenges than opportunities for countering WMD, but the United States can make choices and pursue approaches that mitigate challenges and accentuate opportunities. To that end, the following policy considerations are offered:

- The United States needs to again provide leadership to states that share its values and most important interests and restore their confidence in its commitment to leadership. In a world where U.S. rivals are increasingly powerful and assertive, the United States has greater need for dependable and capable allies and partners. The United States must insist, however, that allies and partners make greater contributions to collective security, and it can do so without alienating them. Providing leadership will help restore allies' and partners' confidence in U.S. security guarantees and will mitigate incentives for them to pursue alternative security arrangements, which for some could include nuclear weapons or other WMD development or hedge programs.

- The United States is right to pursue strategic discussions and negotiations with both Russia and China that cover a broader range of weapons systems and feature strong monitoring and verification provisions. China is becoming too powerful to be left out; it will weigh heavily on strategic discussions and negotiations whether it is at the table or not, so better to find a way to bring it in. The United States, however, will have to be prepared to include systems that are of particular concern to its great power rivals if it is to productively engage those countries. This will take time; in the meantime, the United States should agree to extend the New Strategic Arms Reduction Treaty (New START).

- The United States will need to continue to oppose clear and significant violations of nonproliferation agreements and norms, like those perpetrated by Syria and Russia with their chemical weapons use, to deter further violations and shore up nonproliferation regimes. Violators must be exposed and costs imposed, even if they are unlikely to change those violators' behavior, because the audience also includes other potential violators. Positive responses need to be acknowledged (and rewarded if significant enough) and succor withheld in their absence.

- The United States needs to reevaluate its approach to the North Korean and Iranian nuclear programs. It is increasingly apparent that the United States and like-minded nations are not able to compel or induce North Korea to eliminate a nuclear weapons program that Pyongyang considers essential to its survival. It also is not evident the United States can prevent Iran from acquiring a nuclear weapons capability without the active and coordinated support of other major powers. The United States may need to accord more emphasis to negotiating restrictions on the size and nature of the North Korean program than to insisting on denuclearization. The United States also should refocus on how it can come together with its erstwhile JCPOA partners on a new approach that will provide greater assurance that Iran will never acquire a nuclear weapon. In both cases, the United States will need to continue military and other measures to deter, defend against, and apply pressure to North Korea and Iran in order to move each toward agreement while guarding against the possibility of failure.

- The United States must pay more attention to the dangerous combination of expanding nuclear weapons programs and continuing—and periodically heightening—tensions in South Asia. An India-Pakistan conflict that escalates to the nuclear level not only would be an immense humanitarian and environmental disaster that the United States could not ignore, but it would upset the United States' growing investment in strategic alignment with India, along with Japan and Australia, to balance China's rising power.

- The United States needs to assess whether its expanding resort to financial sanctions in the pursuit of parochial and controversial aims is counterproductive. If other international actors view the United States as abusing its dominant position in the international financial system, they will be more motivated to pursue workarounds to the dollarized economy, which will undermine U.S. financial power over time and the many benefits that arise from such power, including the ability to use that power to counter WMD proliferation. This is already underway. For its own long-term interest, the United States should be more judicious in the use of financial sanctions, applying them for purposes shared by at least our key allies or in defense of critical national interests.

- U.S. leaders need to consider carefully what they are prepared to go to war over with great power rivals and ensure they have the U.S. public's understanding and backing for doing so. This is especially important in the Indo-Pacific theater where the United States faces a rising peer rival in China with near-term designs on territory and waters that are not self-evidently vital to the United States and where geography and new types of conventional weapons may lead one or more great powers to wager that they can fight a war without escalating to the nuclear level.

- The United States must remain at the forefront of developing, utilizing, and understanding the national security implications of emerging or disruptive technologies, such as artificial intelligence, biotechnology, quantum systems, and additive manufacturing, because these technologies may dramatically impact the character of conflict, the economic fortunes of countries, and the balance of power in the international system.

This paper ends with a word on the coronavirus pandemic. The pandemic may provide added motivation to some malign actors for the development and use of biological weapons. At the same time, it has shown that pandemics are as likely to disrupt or even devastate one's friends as one's adversaries. It also has shown how new and emerging scientific and technological capabilities can be exploited to develop medical countermeasures much faster than has been the case in the past. On balance, the net effect of the pandemic on the motivations and ability of malign actors to pursue and use biological weapons may prove to be minor. Less ambiguously, the pandemic has accentuated pre-existing deficiencies in international leadership and cooperation, but these deficiencies are amenable to remedy.

INTRODUCTION

In 2014, the Center for the Study of Weapons of Mass Destruction at National Defense University published a paper on the future of weapons of mass destruction (WMD).[2] It projected WMD-relevant geopolitical and technological trends and made judgments as to how those trends would shape the nature and role of WMD in 2030. Those projections and judgments, summarized in the next section, largely remain viable. Since 2014, however, significant developments bearing on the future of WMD have occurred, which this paper explores.

THE 2014 PAPER

Geopolitically, the 2014 paper projected that the United States would remain the world's most powerful country through 2030 but be less dominant in an increasingly multipolar international system. Non-state groups, potentially including violent extremist organizations, would grow in capabilities and importance. Sources of international conflict would remain and could intensify, and the risks for armed conflict, both inter- and intra-state, would grow. The "battle of narratives" would be an increasingly important part of armed conflict.[3]

Technologically, there would be lower obstacles to the covert development of nuclear weapons and to the development of more sophisticated nuclear weapons. Chemical and biological weapons likely would be 1) more accessible to both state and non-state actors; 2) more capable, particularly in terms of their ability to defeat current and currently emerging defensive countermeasures; 3) more discriminate; that is, more precisely targeted and/or more reliably low- or nonlethal; and 4) harder to attribute (utilizing hitherto unknown agents and/or delivery mechanisms) than the traditional forms known in 2014.

From these projections, the 2014 paper anticipated that longstanding efforts of the international community writ large to exclude WMD from international competition and conflict could be undermined by 2030. Proliferation likely would be harder to prevent and thus potentially more prevalent. Nuclear weapons likely would play a more significant role in the international security environment, and current constraints on the proliferation and use of chemical and biological weapons could weaken. There would be greater scope for WMD terrorism, though it is not possible to predict the frequency or severity of any future employment of WMD. New forms of WMD—beyond chemical, biological, radiological, and nuclear weapons—were unlikely to emerge by 2030, but cyber weapons would probably be capable of inflicting such widespread or severe disruption that the United States may become as reliant on the threat to impose unacceptable costs to deter large-scale cyberattacks as it currently is to deter the use of WMD. The definition of weapons of mass destruction would remain uncertain and controversial in 2030, and its value as an analytic category would be increasingly open to question.[4]

THIS PAPER

Significant geopolitical and technological developments bearing on the future of WMD that have emerged since the 2014 paper or that were largely not addressed in that study include: 1) shifting roles among the great powers; 2) new pressures on arms control and nonproliferation regimes; 3) more roles for chemical and biological weapons; 4) expanding use of U.S. financial sanctions as an instrument of policy; 5) new types of delivery vehicles and more scope to develop and deploy them; and 6) other emerging or disruptive technologies with WMD relevance. To examine these developments, this paper is organized with the following sections:

- *Shifting Roles at the Top* discusses the changing relationships among China, Russia, and the United States and their implications for WMD.

- *Regimes Under Pressure: Nuclear* addresses nuclear arms control and nuclear nonproliferation developments and, in so doing, looks at the evolving nuclear postures of China, India, Iran, North Korea, Pakistan, Russia, and the United States.

- *Regimes Under Pressure: Chemical and Biological* assesses recent chemical weapons use and looks at challenges for chemical and biological weapons nonproliferation, including potential implications of the coronavirus pandemic.

- *Expanding Use of Financial Sanctions* considers the implications of the United States' increasing resort to financial sanctions to advance nonproliferation and other national interests.

- *New Delivery Vehicles* discusses how the end of the Intermediate-Range Nuclear Forces (INF) Treaty, the emergence of new hypersonic and nuclear-powered strike systems, and further development of unmanned systems and remote sensing capabilities may impact strategic competition and prospects for great power war.

- *Other Emerging or Disruptive Technologies* considers WMD implications of artificial intelligence, biotechnology, quantum systems, and additive manufacturing.

- The *Conclusion* summarizes these developments and offers policy considerations going forward.

This paper was finalized in early November 2020 so does not reflect later events like the 2020 U.S. presidential election result.

SHIFTING ROLES AT THE TOP

The post-World War II U.S.-led international security order is being challenged sooner and more aggressively than anticipated in the 2014 paper, and not just by the United States' principal rivals but also as a function of U.S. policy choices. This development is expected to lend more impetus to some other states' consideration of WMD as a security alternative in a more uncertain world.

CHINA

China surpassed the United States in gross domestic product (GDP) measured in purchasing power parity in 2013, and some expect it will overtake the United States in GDP measured in market exchange rates this decade.[5] Other, broader measures of aggregate power, such as a modified version of the Global Power Index developed by RAND, similarly forecast the possibility that China will surpass the United States in a number of key metrics of state power in the years ahead.[6] China may stumble along the way, but no other country currently combines such a large population with sustained economic growth. While the coronavirus pandemic has hurt both the Chinese and U.S. economies, China is likely to have gained further ground on the United States during 2020.[7]

Since Xi Jinping became China's President in 2013, Beijing has more openly displayed its growing power and ambition and has more aggressively asserted its interests than it had prior to his accession. In his landmark address to the 19th Congress of the Chinese Communist Party in October 2017, President Xi laid out ambitious goals for his rising country, including to "become a global leader in terms of composite national strength and international influence" and to develop a "world class military force" by 2050. Xi's report effectively acknowledged what had been increasingly evident for some years: China no longer adheres to the earlier Chinese leader Deng Xiaoping's strategy of "hide our capabilities and bide our time."[8] As one scholar has observed, "In a nutshell, to read [Xi's address to the 19th Party Congress]…is to realize that Beijing's aim is nothing less than preeminent status in the global order."[9]

Under Xi's leadership, China has declared its intent to dominate key technologies of the future, including artificial intelligence, genomics, and quantum computing, and has initiated major investments to that end.[10] China also is extending its influence within and beyond its region through its ambitious Belt and Road Initiative (BRI), which invests in infrastructure projects and special economic zones around the world. Through BRI, China is building and securing access to strategic infrastructure, such as ports in Burma, Sri Lanka, and Pakistan.[11] Xi announced the initiative in 2013. A January 2020 backgrounder by the Council on Foreign Relations (CFR) estimated that China already had spent $200 billion on BRI projects and referenced a Morgan Stanley projection of more than $1 trillion of spending by China over the life of the initiative. Though BRI is derided by critics as promising more than it delivers and saddling beneficiaries with exploitable debt, the CFR report also indicated that more than 60 countries had signed on to BRI projects or indicated an interest in doing so, including some U.S. allies in Europe.[12]

Xi's China is more aggressively asserting its longstanding sovereignty claims in the South and East China Seas. It rejected a 2016 ruling by an international tribunal against its claim to sovereignty over most of the South China Sea on the basis of a Chinese map featuring the "nine-dash-line."[13] It artificially expanded and militarized disputed islets in the Spratly Islands. China's maritime forces and civilian vessels harass and occasionally perpetrate violence against the vessels and crews of regional states in disputed waters. Its civilian vessels, often with naval escorts, conduct commercial activities, such as resource surveying, in the exclusive economic zones claimed by Southeast Asian countries.[14] China's maritime and aviation forces regularly challenge the territorial seas and airspace surrounding the disputed Senkaku Islands that Japan administers.[15] China also makes frequent displays of force in an attempt to intimidate Taiwan and threatens forceful reunification should Taiwan move towards independence.[16]

Lending increasing weight to China's more assertive posture in its region is the steady growth of its military capabilities, the product of an impressive, decades-long modernization effort that Beijing put on display during a military parade on 1 October 2019 marking the 70th anniversary of the founding of the People's Republic of China.[17] As a result, U.S. defense experts are more circumspect about the prospects for U.S. victory in a military conflict with China. The 2018 U.S. National Defense Strategy Commission, for example, assessed that the United States "might struggle to win, or perhaps lose, a war against China or Russia."[18]

RUSSIA

Unlike China, Russia does not threaten to overtake the United States as the world's preeminent power, but it concentrates its more limited economic resources on its military and has more directly challenged the U.S.-led international order.[19] Since 2014, Russia under President Vladimir Putin seized and annexed the Crimean peninsula from Ukraine and initiated and sustained a frozen conflict in eastern Ukraine, adding to those it earlier created in Georgia and Moldova. It intervened militarily in the Syrian civil conflict and eventually enabled the Assad regime to regain control of most of Syria, whereas the United States limited its role to ousting Islamic State from its self-declared caliphate. In so doing, Russia has gained new power and influence in the Middle East at the expense of the United States. It also is playing a major role in the ongoing conflict in Libya, where the United States has absented itself.[20] Russia further intervened in the 2016 U.S. presidential elections to, *inter alia*, exacerbate divisions within the U.S. electorate and did so again in the 2020 elections.[21] It has intervened in European elections, too.[22]

Russia is far along in a broad-scoped reform and modernization of its military, which it initiated after serious deficiencies were exposed during its 2008 intervention in Georgia. The Russian military today is a smaller, more mobile, and balanced force demonstrably capable of projecting power along Russia's periphery and in the Middle East, even if it does not pose as great a threat as the Soviet military did.[23] It is updating and may be expanding its nuclear forces while also developing long-range precision-guided conventional weapons systems.[24] In 2018, President Putin announced the development of five new strategic weapons systems, including a heavy intercontinental ballistic missile; a nuclear-capable, air-launched ballistic missile; a hypersonic glide vehicle; a nuclear-propelled cruise missile; and a nuclear-propelled, nuclear-armed unmanned underwater vehicle.[25]

Nuclear weapons are more central to Russia's military strategy than that of the United States or China. Russia has made nuclear threats against European NATO states and simulated nuclear attacks against NATO targets as part of large-scale military exercises.[26] It has also expressly threatened nuclear attacks against the U.S. homeland.[27] In addition to strategic nuclear forces that overall are on a par with the United States, Russia has long possessed an arsenal of nonstrategic nuclear weapons[28] and dual-capable delivery systems larger than that of its American rival. It is modernizing these systems and adding new types not seen since the Cold War, which the United States worries may reflect a greater willingness by Moscow to resort to limited nuclear strikes during a major conflict.[29] Some believe Russia has an "escalate-to-deescalate" doctrine by which it would initiate limited nuclear strikes with theater systems if losing a regional conventional conflict so as to compel its adversary to back down.[30]

SINO-RUSSIAN STRATEGIC COOPERATION

Growing strategic cooperation between Russia and China against the United States compounds the challenge each poses to the U.S.-led international order. While Sino-Russian relations had improved markedly since the end of the Cold War, including a 1991 agreement resolving their border disputes, cooperation has accelerated since 2014. Their bilateral relationship has focused on increased military cooperation, including arms sales and military exercises; closer economic ties, mainly involving energy; and coordinated responses on international issues,[31] including those concerning North Korea, Iran, Syria, and Venezuela. Russia and China each views the United States as its principal rival and threat, and they share antipathy for the United States' traditional promotion of democracy and human rights and what they hold to be its associated criticism of, and interference in, the sovereign affairs of other states. Notable developments in their bilateral relationship since 2014 include Russia's sale of its advanced S-400 air defense system and Su-35 combat aircraft to China;[32] the participation of Chinese troops in two large-scale Russian military exercises on Russian territory;[33] the first joint, long-range Russian-Chinese air patrol in the Asia-Pacific region, skirting both South Korean and Japanese airspace;[34] and Chinese President Xi's referral to Russian President Putin as his "best friend."[35]

Russia and China's strategic cooperation against the United States fits a realist's balance of power paradigm where lesser states align to offset the system's dominant power. Most analysts do not expect Russia and China's strategic alignment to progress to a formal military alliance, though.[36] Neither state is under sufficient direct threat to require the protection of a formal security pact, while the establishment of such an alliance could impede the ability of each to work with the United States and its allies in areas of common interest. Divergent interests also serve as a brake on a formal alliance, particularly Russia's unwillingness to be perceived as the junior partner and its suspicions of how China's ambitions may expand as its power grows.[37] On 22 October 2020, Putin said about a military alliance with China, "We don't need it, but theoretically it's quite possible to imagine it."[38] Strategic alignment serves both countries' interests for now in constraining their shared U.S. rival and is likely to endure through 2030.

UNITED STATES

China and Russia are not the only disruptors of the post–World War II international order. The 2016 U.S. presidential election produced a new U.S. approach to international relations. The resultant administration criticized the international trade system and U.S. allies for taking advantage of the United States, opposed various aspects of globalization, and called on states always to put their own interests first.[39] Yet, the administration's National Security Strategy and National Defense Strategy also reinforced the need for a strong framework of allies and partners to compete with revisionist states and ensure military advantage.[40] The ensuing mismatch of strategy, action, and rhetoric has led to confusion and doubt among traditional U.S. allies and partners, weakened Western cohesion, and possibly emboldened or created opportunities for adversaries.

The United States withdrew support or forced renegotiation of major international trade agreements or mechanisms, including the Trans-Pacific Partnership (withdrew), North American Free Trade Agreement (renegotiated and replaced by the U.S.-Mexico-Canada Agreement), U.S.-Republic of Korea (ROK) Free Trade Agreement (renegotiated), and Appellate Body of the World Trade Organization (denied its ability to function by blocking the filling of vacancies[41]). The United States also made unprecedented use of tariff authorities in recent years, wielding them against friends and rivals alike to extract economic concessions, especially against China, but also broadly on a number of others states with regard to steel, aluminum, and other products.[42]

The value of U.S. alliances, particularly NATO and the U.S.-ROK alliance, was questioned, and greater allied financial contributions to those security relationships more forcibly demanded.[43] The European Union (EU) and major European allies, especially Germany, were characterized at times more as economic competitors than as security allies.[44] In June 2020, a major reduction in the U.S. force presence in Germany was announced and attributed to Germany's deficient defense spending.[45] The United States broke with allies and other Western states to effectively end its participation in the Paris Climate Agreement and to withdraw from the JCPOA on the Iranian nuclear program. Admiration and empathy were expressed at times for leaders of illiberal regimes that threaten or challenge the integrity of U.S. alliances, including Russian President Putin, Chinese President Xi, North Korean Chairman Kim Jong Un, Hungarian Prime Minister Viktor Orban, and Turkish President Recep Tayyip Erdogan.[46]

Disruptive views expressed by top political leadership have been variable, though, and, in some cases, apparently at odds with more traditional policies articulated and executed by U.S. departments and agencies. For example, top political leadership initially described NATO as obsolete and did not affirm its

Article 5 mutual defense guarantee, but more traditional positions were reaffirmed later.[47] Expressions of admiration and empathy for illiberal world leaders sit awkwardly with U.S. actions, some required by law, punishing those leaders' regimes, such as tariffs against China for predatory economic practices, sanctions against Russia for its intervention in Ukraine, and sanctions against Turkey for procuring the Russian S-400 air defense system. The result is uncertainty about the true direction and durability of U.S. policy.

Most recently, the United States declined to provide the global leadership in responding to the novel coronavirus pandemic that it had in the 2008 global financial crisis and the 2014-16 Ebola outbreak in West Africa. In 2008, the United States created and utilized the G20 group of nations and worked closely with multilateral organizations, like the International Monetary Fund, in responding to the global financial crisis.[48] During the 2014-16 Ebola outbreak, the United States worked closely with affected countries, European allies, and the World Health Organization (WHO) in coordinating the response.[49] In 2020, neither the G20 nor the smaller G7 group of leading Western nations has figured prominently in the pandemic response.[50] The United States also announced its intent to withdraw from the WHO for that organization's failures in responding to the pandemic and "alarming lack of independence" from China.[51] The United States further chose not to participate in an effort (COVAX) involving roughly 150 nations to develop, manufacture, and distribute coronavirus vaccine, at least in part because it is co-led by the WHO.[52]

The lack of U.S. leadership on the 2020 pandemic response has been conspicuous and much commented upon.[53] German Foreign Minister Heiko Maas warned in April 2020, with regard to the United States' withdrawal from the WHO, "Every inch that the U.S. withdraws from the wider world, especially at this level, is space that will be occupied by others—and that tends to be those that don't share our values of liberal democracy."[54] Public polling of Americans, French, and Germans done jointly by the Bertelsmann Foundation, The German Marshall Fund of the United States, and Institut Montaigne in January and May 2020 indicated a significant decrease in perceptions of the United States as the world's most influential nation and a larger increase in perceptions of China in that regard, though the United States still remained on top.[55]

The purpose of the above delineation of U.S. statements and actions in recent years is not to judge their appropriateness or efficacy; rather, it is to demonstrate that they represent a significant departure from the U.S. policy and practice of exercising and bearing the costs of leadership of the liberal, rules-based international order established at the end of World War II. It is not that prior U.S. administrations had not challenged or undermined significant aspects of that order; e.g., the Nixon administration abandoned the gold standard that hitherto had underpinned the international monetary system. However, none has done so across such a broad front, so aggressively, and as part of an explicit philosophy of nationalist self-interest. There are valid arguments for and against the new directions taken by the United States in recent years, but few will argue that they are not significant and that they stand to be much more so if continued.

It is not entirely clear to what extent the United States' current disruptive approach to the international order is more the product of one administration's unique views and way of conducting itself or of larger forces within the United States and abroad. If more of the former, some reversion to the mean is likely in successor administrations, but if more of the latter, a disruptive approach likely will endure or even intensify in some form beyond the Trump administration's tenure.

A harder line toward China is most likely to endure, as it has broad and bipartisan support among the U.S. polity, but that is not necessarily inconsistent with a renewed U.S. leadership role for a liberal, rules-based international order. The Soviet challenge galvanized U.S. leadership of the Western world during the Cold War, and a strong majority of Americans still consider NATO important for their security.[56] Other realities, however, militate against such a leadership imperative over time, particularly the nation's high debt, exacerbated by the fiscal response to the 2020 pandemic; an inward-looking tendency of the progressive wing of the Democratic Party and the libertarian wing of the Republican party, if not to the same purposes; and broader weariness with the high costs and meager returns from nearly two decades of conflict in the Middle East and Afghanistan.

Because of these factors and the shift in relative power among the United States, China, and Russia discussed earlier, it is now more likely than anticipated in the 2014 paper that the United States will be less able, and perhaps less willing, than it was under earlier administrations to exercise international leadership and to dependably extend security guarantees to allies and partners, regardless of the identity of the next several U.S. presidents. As two British scholars observed about the United States' closest allied relationship, "The UK's relationship with the US is now less reliable than at any time over the last half-century … it would be complacent to assume that relations with the US could easily revert to where they were before."[57] As there are no good alternatives to U.S. leadership in the foreseeable future, though, future U.S. administrations will need to offer leadership and make the case for doing so to the U.S. public, and allies and partners will need to bolster the case by making greater contributions to the common defense.

IMPLICATIONS FOR WMD

If the United States steps away from its leadership of the Western group of nations and its other security partners at the same time that China and Russia are asserting their power,[58] then the proliferation and use of WMD may become significantly less constrained in the new order that emerges—and sooner than anticipated in the 2014 paper. U.S. protection, extended deterrence guarantees, and defense agreements have long enabled many of its allies and partners to forswear WMD capabilities. Some may soon pursue their own nuclear weapons rather than continue to rely upon the protection of a less committed United States in a more uncertain international security environment.[59] Some U.S. allies and partners are likely to recall comments during the 2016 presidential election that more countries, including U.S. allies and partners, may need to acquire their own nuclear weapons given nuclear proliferation in their regions and the inability or unwillingness of the United States to continue to bear the costs of protecting them.[60]

In 2018, Saudi Crown Prince Muhammed bin Salman stated that Saudi Arabia would acquire its own nuclear weapons should Iran do so.[61] Saudi Arabia, which intends to build nuclear reactors to generate power, has resisted U.S. pressure to foreswear uranium enrichment and plutonium reprocessing capabilities and to conclude an enhanced safeguards agreement (Additional Protocol) with the International Atomic Energy Agency.[62] In 2019, Turkish President Erdogan said it is unacceptable that some states can have nuclear weapons and Turkey cannot.[63] Polling has indicated over the past few years that a majority of South Koreans support either the return of U.S. nuclear weapons to their country or the development of their own nuclear weapons.[64]

Usually without reference to nuclear weapons, leaders of some prominent European states and numerous European security experts have spoken with greater urgency over the last three years on the need for Europe to reduce its reliance upon the United States for security. A few, however, have raised the possibility of a European nuclear deterrent.[65] That almost certainly would require a larger role for France's nuclear force beyond just defending itself, particularly now that the United Kingdom has left the European Union. It also is worth recalling that the Federal Republic of Germany (FRG), the Cold War predecessor to the current German state, sought assurance from the United States during the negotiation of the Nuclear Non-Proliferation Treaty (NPT) that it would consider the FRG to have adequate reason to withdraw from the NPT in the event that the U.S. security guarantee to NATO ended.[66]

Also without reference to nuclear weapons, recent Japanese Prime Minister Shinzo Abe persevered in his efforts to accord to the Japanese Self-Defense Forces the same role that militaries play in other democracies and made progress in that regard.[67] His goal most likely was to strengthen his country's alliance with the United States against threats from China and North Korea by demonstrating that Japan can make a larger contribution to the common defense. Nonetheless, Japan's possession of the largest store of fissile material of any U.S. ally or partner who is not a nuclear weapons state is an ace card available to Tokyo in case of sufficiently deteriorating security circumstances. Continuity is expected from Abe's close ally and successor as prime minister, Yoshihide Suga.[68] For its part, Australia, in its *2020 Defence Strategic Update*, reiterated its dependence upon U.S. nuclear and conventional capabilities to offer effective deterrence against potential nuclear threats to Australia, but added new language on Australia's need to take "greater responsibility" for its own security and to "grow its self-reliant ability to deliver deterrent effects."[69]

Acquiring nuclear weapons, or even other forms of WMD enabled by new technologies, is not the only or necessarily the preferred means for U.S. allies and partners to ensure their security in a more uncertain international security environment. Most presumably would prefer to reinforce their security bonds with the United States, given the economic and political costs of attempting to replace that security on their own.[70] That is likely an important reason why a number of NATO allies have been responsive to intensified U.S. demands for greater defense spending. Other options available to allies and security partners are to balance with other countries against common rivals (though few other countries can or are willing to extend a nuclear deterrent to an ally) or to accommodate the interests and demands of their rivals. But those options may not be available or palatable, and when that is the case, the possession of nuclear weapons and potentially other WMD is a unilateral alternative, and one especially accessible to advanced industrial states.

REGIMES UNDER PRESSURE: NUCLEAR

Pillars of nuclear arms control and nonproliferation have fallen or become wobbly since the 2014 paper, endangering their contribution to mitigating the threats of WMD.

NUCLEAR ARMS CONTROL

The United States followed by Russia withdrew from the Intermediate-Range Nuclear Forces (INF) Treaty[71] in 2019. The United States' withdrawal was precipitated by Russia's refusal, after years of discussion, to acknowledge much less rectify its testing of the 9M729 (SCC-8) ground-launched cruise missile in excess of the ranges permitted by the treaty.[72] In May 2020, the United States announced it would withdraw in six months from the Open Skies Treaty[73] in response to a history of Russian violations, unless Russia returned to compliance.[74] Recent expressions of U.S. suspicion that Russia and China have conducted very low-yield nuclear tests in contravention of the broadly-accepted U.S. "zero-yield" standard under the Comprehensive Test Ban Treaty (CTBT),[75] followed by reports that senior U.S. officials have discussed the possibility of resuming U.S. nuclear testing,[76] also have raised concerns about the future of that accord (which the United States has signed but not ratified) and nuclear testing moratoria.

The New Strategic Arms Reduction Treaty[77] is the last standing pillar of U.S.-Russian nuclear arms control,[78] and it will expire in February 2021 unless both the United States and Russia exercise the option to extend it for up to five years.[79] Russia had called for New START's extension without conditions,[80] but the United States had sought assurances that a new agreement will be negotiated that includes China and controls a broader range of nuclear weapons.[81] In October 2020, there were indications that the United States and Russia were discussing a one-year extension of the treaty with a politically-binding freeze on the number of nuclear weapons.[82] If New START expires without replacement, it will be the first time since 1972 that there will be no international legal constraint on the size and composition of key elements of the U.S. and Russian nuclear forces.[83] This would reduce transparency and predictability in the U.S.-Russian strategic nuclear balance. It could even precipitate a significant change in the size and composition of the U.S. and Russian nuclear arsenals and spur a compensating change in China's nuclear posture.

United States

In 2020, the United States identified two general concerns with the existing New START agreement which it seeks to address via trilateral arms control.[84] First is the ongoing expansion of the Russian and Chinese arsenals, which contrasts with no growth in the U.S. nuclear force. U.S. officials have said that the expansion of the Russian arsenal is occurring primarily in nonstrategic nuclear weapons (NSNW), which are not subject to controls under New START or any other formal agreement,[85] and new strategic delivery vehicles under development, only some of which would be accountable under New START rules (if still in force) as they are deployed.[86] China, which is not a party to New START, is building a range of new strategic and nonstrategic delivery systems, including heavy intercontinental ballistic missiles (ICBMs), hypersonic delivery vehicles, a new ballistic missile submarine, an air-launched ballistic missile, and other generally theater-range missiles capable of carrying nuclear or conventional warheads. China is expected to double the size of its nuclear warhead arsenal this decade, according to U.S. Department of Defense (DoD) estimates.[87]

The second U.S. concern is with transparency and future compliance. While the United States considers Russia to be in compliance with New START,[88] a senior U.S. official said that the treaty has verification weaknesses and expressed concern about Russia's history of violating other arms control and security agreements, including the INF and Open Skies treaties.[89] This official identified those New START verification weaknesses as including the absence of a requirement for Russia to provide telemetry on strategic systems under development and too much time between when the United States requests an onsite inspection and when Russia is required to allow the U.S. inspectors access to the site.[90] In the case of China, the issue is the opacity of all aspects of its nuclear posture, including systems and doctrine. China is not party to any agreement obligating it to provide to the United States information on, and access to, its strategic forces, nor does it volunteer any. China has repeatedly rebuffed U.S invitations to discuss matters bearing on its strategic forces.[91] Chinese officials reportedly view nuclear transparency as a tool of the strong (the United States) to bully or maintain advantage over the weak (China).[92]

Russia

Russia has its own concerns and goals for nuclear arms control. It fears that the United States aims to defeat its nuclear deterrent through integrating national and theater missile defenses and conventional prompt strike systems and wants these U.S. capabilities limited.[93] The United States has been unwilling to consider limitations on its missile defense systems as part of formal arms control agreements with Russia; it insists that its missile defense posture is geared only toward, and effective against, the smaller ballistic missile forces of North Korea and Iran.[94] A related Russian concern is that the United States intends to place missile defense sensors and interceptors, and perhaps even conventionally armed land attack systems, in space.[95] In 2008, Russia and China proposed to the United Nations a treaty to ban the placement of all weapons in outer space (existing treaties only ban nuclear weapons and tests in outer space, and all weapons only on celestial bodies), and they continue to advocate for it.[96] The United States opposes Russia and China's proposed space treaty, most importantly because it does not limit ground-based anti-satellite weapons, like the kind that Russia and China possess, which the United States currently considers to be the greatest threat to satellites (though it is increasingly concerned about Russian "interceptor" satellites functioning as weapons against other satellites).[97]

Russia has expressed little interest in U.S. efforts over time to set limits on nonstrategic nuclear weapons and has said that the United States first needed to remove its own weapons from Europe. As noted earlier, Russia possesses many more and a greater variety of nonstrategic nuclear weapons than does the United States, and these weapons play a larger role in Russia's nuclear doctrine than they do in U.S. concepts and plans.[98]

If New START expires, Russia would be able to exceed the agreement's limits on strategic offensive nuclear forces more quickly than would the United States. While both Russia and the United States have warheads in storage that could be uploaded on existing delivery systems, Russia is currently producing nuclear warheads and delivery systems while the United States is not. The Kremlin also would not have to contend with the type of domestic opposition that a U.S. administration would encounter if it moved to expand the U.S. nuclear arsenal.[99]

Yet it is Russia that is calling for the extension of New START and the United States that has been reluctant. While Russia might reap political utility from achieving a quantitatively-superior nuclear force, in that quantitative superiority could complicate U.S. relationships with some allies to whom the U.S. extends deterrence, Russia likely understands that such a force would not deny the United States a secure, second-strike capability[100] and may complicate Moscow's relationship with China. Russia also likely appreciates that it cannot afford to compete with the United States (or China) if an arms race did ensue over the longer term. Moreover, Russia already is enhancing its nuclear arsenal in areas that are not accountable under New START. Such factors could explain why Russia prefers the stability of extending New START to the risks and costs of seeing it expire and suggests it would be a willing party to the negotiation of a follow-on accord.

Moscow previously has acknowledged a need for multilateral nuclear arms control but has been cool to the United States' recent call for a trilateral engagement with China and has dismissed the U.S. contention that Russia needed to help bring China to the table.[101] While it is conceivable that Russia would welcome China's participation, Beijing has flatly refused to do so, and Russia is unwilling to antagonize the Chinese on the matter.[102] Moreover, Russia already has agreements with China that afford it more insight than the United States into Chinese military activities and capabilities, including on ballistic missile launches.[103] Russia also has said that France and the United Kingdom would have to be part of multilateral nuclear arms control.[104]

China

China apparently sees little or no benefit in subjecting itself to the transparency and limitations of nuclear arms control at this time. It holds that there is no basis for it to participate as long as the U.S. and Russian nuclear arsenals remain much larger than its own.[105] While the U.S. Office of the Secretary of Defense projects China's nuclear warhead stockpile to at least double in size over the next decade, that would still leave it at only a quarter of the level of the deployed strategic warheads (let alone non-deployed and tactical warheads) permitted to the United States and Russia under the New START treaty.[106] Beijing also points to its long-established policy of no first-use of nuclear weapons and eschewing nuclear arms racing as demonstrating that it is a responsible nuclear power. China concluded long ago that it did not require nuclear parity with the United States and Russia to deter nuclear attack and coercion and built a smaller and more affordable force. It is adapting that force now to the evolving strategic environment, particularly the more precise strike systems and improving missile defenses of the United States, by making its arsenal larger, more capable, and more survivable.[107] While China may continue to eschew quantitative nuclear parity with the United States and Russia, it also may be loath to lock in such asymmetry in a formal agreement.[108]

Could China be induced to engage in trilateral nuclear arms control? When that question was put to the U.S. special envoy for arms control in May 2020, his response was two-fold: First, China, as one of the five nuclear weapons states recognized by the Nuclear Non-Proliferation Treaty, has an obligation to negotiate over its nuclear forces. If China fails to honor this obligation, the United States is prepared to take unspecified economic or defense measures to affect China's calculus. Second, China should welcome the opportunity that joining the United States and Russia at the nuclear negotiating table affords to demonstrate the great power status that Beijing desires.[109] It is not evident that these considerations will motivate China to engage in nuclear arms control with the United States and Russia. China's NPT obligations have existed since it joined the treaty in 1992. It increasingly is recognized as a great power despite it not engaging in nuclear arms control. China also already is the subject of punitive and coercive economic pressure from the United States, and China's growing military might is the primary justification for recently enacted and requested U.S. defense budget increases.

Implications for Nuclear Arms Control Going Forward

The context for nuclear arms control is quite different going forward than what had transpired before, and China is an important reason why. Nuclear arms control has been bilateral for most of its history, not only because the United States and Russia had by far the largest and most consequential nuclear arsenals, but also because each was the other's greatest security threat. That was true even during the United States' "unipolar moment" after the Cold War ended because Russia still possessed the only nuclear arsenal comparable to that of the United States, and China's military challenge at the time was more potential than realized. Now, though, China generally is recognized to be the world's second leading power and is closing the gap with the United States, while Russia, though militarily more capable and daring than during its 1990s nadir, is expected to slip further behind China and the United States in the years to come. Whether or not China sits at the negotiating table, it will weigh far more heavily in the calculations of those that would, especially the United States, than was the case in the past.

China, however, is only one of the factors that is making nuclear arms control more complex and harder to achieve, yet probably more important, than in the past. As will be discussed more below, technological developments are enabling new nuclear and conventional weapons and supporting systems, such as hypersonic missiles and more ubiquitous sensors, which will operate in and across more domains, including space and cyberspace. The reach, speed, and precision of new delivery systems and often their ability to be fitted with nuclear or conventional payloads will blur thresholds separating nuclear and conventional systems as well as the strategic and operational levels of conflict. More precise conventionally armed weapons systems are gaining the ability to execute missions formerly restricted to nuclear weapons and are becoming more integrated (by design or de facto) with nuclear weapons systems in states' deployments and operations. Escalation challenges accordingly will be exacerbated. In addition, it is reasonable to expect that India (discussed more in the next section) will bear more on the calculus of the great powers and eventually become one of them, though not during this decade.

In this more complex geopolitical and technological environment, nuclear arms control will increasingly need to be about both nuclear and advanced conventional capabilities. It also will need to consider the capabilities and interests of more actors, whether or not all of those actors agree to participate. Such strategic arms control will be increasingly important for instilling a measure of transparency, restraint, predictability, and stability to a complex international security order, but it also will be correspondingly harder to achieve. If not achieved, there will be more pressure upon the great powers (and those who aspire to be great powers) to conduct and act on worse-case planning, which could heighten tensions and the likelihood of conflict among them, while reducing the resources that each can invest in meeting pressing non-military needs.

NUCLEAR NONPROLIFERATION

The apparent retreat from nuclear arms control discussed above is one of a series of developments in recent years that have complicated the international community's ability to work together to prevent the further proliferation of nuclear weapons. Others include the United States' withdrawal from the multilateral JCPOA on Iran's nuclear program; the lack of progress in U.S.-North Korean denuclearization negotiations; the expansion of South Asian nuclear arsenals; the upcoming entry into force of the Treaty to Prohibit Nuclear Weapons; and, as already discussed, shifting great power dynamics that may foster proliferation.

Iran

The JCPOA was concluded in 2015 among China, the European Union, France, Germany, Iran, Russia, the United Kingdom, and the United States. It limits Iran's ability to produce fissile material through a set of physical constraints and intrusive monitoring and verification measures. The agreement also reaffirms Iran's existing NPT commitment never to acquire nuclear weapons. The JCPOA, however, allows Iran to retain a substantial nuclear infrastructure and the capacity to expand its enrichment program after the physical constraints on fissile material production and most of the verification and enforcement provisions expire in 10 to 15 years from the accord's start.[110] Most importantly for Iran, the JCPOA resulted in the lifting of more than a decade's worth of accumulated sanctions directly related to its nuclear program.

Iran, an NPT member, has consistently stated that it has no intention of developing nuclear weapons.[111] In 2002, however, the International Atomic Energy Agency (IAEA) began to investigate reports of undeclared Iranian nuclear activities at Natanz and Arak. The next year, the IAEA concluded that Iran had indeed engaged in a variety of clandestine nuclear-related activities, some of which violated Iran's safeguards agreement with the agency. In 2005, the IAEA adopted a formal resolution finding Iran to be in non-compliance with its safeguards agreement. The following year, the IAEA referred the matter to the United Nations Security Council (UNSC).[112] In 2007, the United States released an intelligence assessment indicating that Iranian military entities had been working to develop nuclear weapons until fall 2003, and that these entities were continuing to develop a range of technical capabilities (including Iran's civilian uranium enrichment program) that could be applied to producing nuclear weapons, if a decision was made to do so.[113] The UNSC adopted six resolutions between 2006 and 2010 demanding Iran suspend its uranium enrichment program and undertake several confidence-building measures to address the IAEA's concerns, including with regard to the reported military dimensions of Iran's nuclear work.[114]

Iran has the largest and most diverse missile force in the Middle East, which could provide the means to deliver nuclear weapons if Iran acquires them. Iran's missile force includes hundreds of short- and medium-range ballistic missiles. It also is acquiring land-attack cruise missiles and developing space-launch vehicles with direct relevance to the development of longer-range ballistic missiles if Iran moves in that direction.[115]

When the JCPOA was agreed to in 2015, it was widely viewed as a mixed but net positive development for nuclear nonproliferation and regional stability; however, it also had numerous and influential detractors, particularly hard-liners in Iran and Israel and conservatives in the United States.[116] Principal objections to the JCPOA included its retention of Iran's uranium enrichment infrastructure; the temporary nature of its restrictions on Iran's ability to enrich uranium and to acquire conventional arms from abroad; and the absence of restrictions on Iran's destabilizing activities in the region, including interference in Iraq and support for the Syrian regime, Hizballah, Hamas, and the Houthis.[117] It also did not significantly constrain Iran's missile program.[118]

The United States withdrew from the JCPOA in 2018 notwithstanding Iran's compliance with the agreement at the time, as certified by the IAEA,[119] and the opposition of the accord's other parties.[120] The United States also renewed unilateral economic sanctions and political pressure with the expressed aim of inducing Iran to negotiate a much broader and more restrictive agreement.[121] However, the United States subsequently was unsuccessful in persuading other UNSC members to extend an international arms embargo on Iran[122], and, failing that, to accept the United States' standing to be able to "snap back" UN sanctions on Iran that had been waived pursuant to UNSC 2231.[123]

Renewed U.S. sanctions are having a highly adverse impact on Iran's economy, not least because of the reluctant compliance of non-U.S. and mainly Western firms who fear being punished by Washington despite their own governments' continued support for the JCPOA and largely unsuccessful efforts to establish sanctions workarounds.[124] The United States' unilateral pressure campaign, however, has had less success in ostracizing and politically isolating Iran than when all of the world's leading nations were aligned against Iran's nuclear program prior to the U.S. withdrawal from JCPOA.

Since the U.S. withdrawal, Iran has progressively exceeded JCPOA limits on its nuclear program. According to a September 2020 Institute for Science and International Security estimate, Iran's low enriched uranium (LEU) stock was ten times more than the JCPOA limit. Whereas the JCPOA was designed to keep

Iran at least one year away from being able to produce enough weapons-grade uranium for one nuclear weapon, in its lapse, Iran may be able to produce that much weapons-grade uranium within three and a half months, and a second weapon two months later.[125] In January 2020, Iranian Foreign Minister Javad Zarif threatened that Iran would withdraw from the NPT if the Europeans refer Iran's violations of the JCPOA limits to the United Nations Security Council.[126] Iran apparently seeks to demonstrate that the United States' actions undermine the accord's goal of preventing it from developing nuclear weapons while at the same time keeping the other parties motivated to find a way to blunt the impact of U.S. sanctions. Iran also may hope for a new U.S. administration in 2021 that will return the United States to the JCPOA and reverse or at least ease the recent re-imposition of U.S. sanctions.[127]

If Iran continues to move closer to being able to build a nuclear weapon, covert action against Iran's nuclear program may intensify. A series of incidents impacting Iranian infrastructure during 2020, including a fire at a facility at Natanz that produces centrifuges, raised suspicions that they were acts of sabotage.[128] The Iranian nuclear program long has been the object of suspected acts of sabotage, including the Stuxnet computer worm attack launched in 2009[129] and the assassination of Iranian scientists during 2010-12.[130] It also is prudent to anticipate that Iran's regional rivals will pursue their own countermeasures, which may include developing or otherwise arranging to acquire their own nuclear weapons capabilities. As previously discussed, Saudi Crown Prince Salman has bluntly stated that his country will acquire its own nuclear weapons if Iran does, and Turkish President Erdogan has implied that he may not continue to abide by the NPT's prohibition on acquiring nuclear weapons if others do not. It is possible that Iran will refrain from building a nuclear weapon, even if poised to do so, or at least not do so openly to forestall regional rivals acquiring their own.

North Korea

Since the 2014 paper, the estimated size of North Korea's nuclear arsenal has grown from as few as 10 weapons to more than 50 in 2020.[131] Pyongyang conducted three additional nuclear weapons tests, each with greater magnitude and yield than the one before.[132] Some experts estimated that the most recent test (September 2017) produced a yield of around 100 kilotons; North Korea claimed it was a test of a hydrogen bomb, though it could have been of a boosted fission weapon.[133]

Pyongyang also expanded the size, reach, diversity, survivability, and reliability of its ballistic missile force. During 2016 and 2017, it conducted over 40 launches of short-, medium-, intermediate-, intercontinental-range, and submarine-launched ballistic missile systems.[134] It is reported to have miniaturized nuclear devices that likely fit across the spectrum of its ballistic missiles and that also could allow for the incorporation of penetration aids or the development of multiple warhead systems.[135] It also is fielding mobile missiles and has demonstrated a maneuvering warhead capability.[136] In October 2020, it displayed at a military parade a previously-unseen mobile ICBM which, if real, will be its largest.[137] These developments indicate that North Korea is pursuing a nuclear-armed ballistic missile force that can survive preemptive attacks and overcome missile defense systems.[138] They also suggest North Korea is not only acquiring the means to put the United States at risk, but also options to conduct limited nuclear strikes within its region.[139]

North Korea's nuclear weapon and ballistic missile activities and its bellicose rhetoric fed increasing tensions with the United States at the end of the Obama and beginning of the Trump administrations, to the point where there was active talk of war in 2017. In contrast to its consistently coercive policy toward Iran, however, the Trump administration pivoted from an initially intimidating approach to North Korea toward a more conciliatory one in its effort to persuade Pyongyang to halt and reverse its WMD programs.[140] President Trump became the first U.S. president to meet with his North Korean counterpart; they met a total of three times from June 2018 to June 2019.

Following their initial meeting in Singapore in June 2018, President Trump and Chairman Kim issued a statement that, *inter alia*, reaffirmed prior commitments to denuclearize the Korean peninsula.[141] Yet North Korea and the United States appear to have had different interpretations of the term "denuclearization" where North Korea's concept includes withdrawing the U.S. nuclear umbrella from South Korea.[142] Moreover, North Korea reportedly expected significant sanctions relief in advance of taking major denuclearization measures, which the United States was unwilling to provide.[143] Subsequent negotiations quickly bogged down over such differences and the two later summit meetings did not get them back on track.

North Korea has continued to abide in practice, as of the time of this writing, with its April 2018 moratoria on nuclear tests and launches of long-range ballistic missiles—activities of greatest concern to the United States as they pose the most direct threat to it.[144] In 2019, however, North Korea resumed launches of short-range ballistic missiles and rockets, including new types; tested a new submarine-launched ballistic missile; and displayed a submarine under construction that might carry ballistic missiles. It also continued maintenance and construction on its nuclear facilities.[145] In 2020, Pyongyang conducted additional short-range missile and rocket tests, and North Korean leaders spoke of expanding their nuclear weapons program.[146] Despite optimistic statements by U.S. leaders, North Korea has indicated it is not interested in resuming negotiations with the United States until Washington changes its approach on sanctions relief.[147]

It is becoming ever harder to imagine that Pyongyang will agree to surrender its hard-earned nuclear arsenal absent a fundamental change in the regime and/or geostrategic circumstances. Like other states determined to acquire nuclear weapons to address an external threat perceived as existential (e.g., Pakistan), North Korea will hold on to its weapons to deter attack and withstand intimidation. The Kim regime may negotiate limits on its nuclear arsenal for economic and political gain but is unlikely to countenance denuclearization as that term is understood by the United States.[148] If there ever had been a window to negotiate the end of the Kim regime's nuclear weapons program, it most likely has closed. This suggests that the U.S. imperative is deterrence, and its fundamental policy choice is between maximizing pressure to precipitate regime change and offering inducements to negotiate nuclear limitations.

South Asia

South Asia also is a source of new as well as continuing concerns about nuclear proliferation and use. New concerns are more a matter of vertical than horizontal proliferation. Continuing concerns involve the security of nuclear weapons in the region and longstanding enmity and periodic border clashes between

India and Pakistan that could escalate to a nuclear confrontation.[149] India and China also recently have clashed again along their disputed border,[150] though it is less likely that those clashes would rise to the level of nuclear confrontation.

Since 2015, India has added 40-50 nuclear warheads to its arsenal for an estimated total of 150.[151] While fighter-bombers remain prominent among India's nuclear weapons delivery vehicles, modernization efforts concentrate on missiles, with an emphasis on longer range and sea-based systems that indicate more attention to China than to Pakistan. In terms of land-based ballistic missiles, India completed testing on its IRBM (Agni-IV), conducted further tests of its first ICBM (Agni-V), and began development of an even longer-range ICBM (Agni-VI with range of 8,000-10,000 kilometers). It fielded a ballistic missile submarine (*Arihant* SSBN) and submarine-launched ballistic missile (K-15 SLBM), plans to build additional SSBNs, and is developing a second type of SLBM (K-4 with 3,500 kilometers range). India also operates a short-range, nuclear-armed ballistic missile (*Danush*) from surface ships and is developing a potentially dual-capable cruise missile (*Nirbhay* with 1,000 kilometer range) with ground, air, and sea-launched variants.[152] There are reports that the air variant of India's current *BrahMos* cruise missile may get a nuclear payload and operate with India's new Su-30 fighters.[153]

A 2018 estimate of Pakistan's nuclear arsenal put the number of warheads at 140-150, 20-40 more than was estimated in 2015.[154] Land-based missiles are the mainstay of Pakistan's nuclear weapons delivery vehicles, but Islamabad also utilizes fighter-bomber aircraft and is developing both a sea- and air-launched variant of its *Babur* ground-launched cruise missile. Pakistan operates six short- and medium-range, land-based ballistic missile systems, the latter of which can range all of India and is developing several others.[155] In 2017, Islamabad tested a new land-based MRBM (*Ababeel*) said to be capable of delivering multiple warheads.[156]

If one of the most notable aspects of India's modernization efforts is the increasing range of its missiles, it is the very short range of Pakistan's Nasr ballistic missile that garners particular attention. Ranging only 60 kilometers, Nasr cannot reach significant targets in India; rather, it would target Indian conventional forces invading Pakistan with low-yield nuclear weapons. The Nasr is understood to be a response to India's "Cold Start" strategy, wherein India's army would be poised to quickly take a fight into Pakistan in an effort to deter Pakistani provocations.[157] Pakistan, which has not foresworn the first use of nuclear weapons, aims to deter India by holding battlefield targets at risk with tactical weapons and strategic ones with longer-range systems. Critics, including the United States government, fear that forward-deployed weapons will be less secure and more readily employed during conflict.[158]

Aspects of India's nuclear posture also are generating concern. In 1998, the Indian government released a "draft" nuclear doctrine of no first use (NFU) and "credible minimum deterrence." Though "credible minimum deterrence" was vaguely defined, it was generally understood, like China's nuclear doctrine, to emphasize countervalue vice counterforce capabilities and to minimize nuclear armaments. Yet, again like China, subsequent rhetoric and investments by Indian leaders concerning their nuclear force have led some, including in Pakistan, to wonder if India is moving away from NFU and toward a more counterforce-capable posture. In terms of rhetoric, India's Ministry of External Affairs caveated the NFU policy in 2003 to allow for nuclear weapons use to protect Indian forces operating in Pakistan as well as in response to biological or chemical attack. In August 2019, India's Minister of Defense, Rajnath Singh, implied during remarks at India's Pokran nuclear test site that India would not abide by NFU indefinitely.[159] In terms of investments, India's creation of a submarine nuclear ballistic missile force, fielding of a two-tiered missile defense system, testing of an anti-satellite weapon, use of a sealed-canister launch system for the mobile Agni-V ICBM under development (which enables faster firing of the missile), and interest in multiple independently-targeted reentry vehicle (MIRV) technology are viewed in Pakistan as threats to its nuclear deterrent, even if India undertook them mainly in response to China's nuclear modernization.[160]

There does appear to be a dynamic within what Lori Saalman refers to as the "South Asia nuclear triangle" (China, India, and Pakistan) where one actor's reactions to a second one's activities leads to countervailing reactions by the third actor, even if the third actor is not the intended target.[161] The triangle also could be viewed as a quadrilateral or even a pentagon because it involves the United States and, to a lesser degree, Russia. As Toby Dalton and Tony Zhao describe, China's nuclear activities are largely in response to those of the United States and perhaps also in part to Russia's. Chinese experts largely are dismissive of India's nuclear developments, not considering them a significant threat to their country. India, on the other hand, views China as a threat and follows its nuclear developments closely.[162] When China modernizes its nuclear force in response to U.S. developments, like missile defense and conventional prompt strike, India perceives a requirement for compensating changes to its posture, like those identified in the above paragraph. (Of course, some Chinese actions more directly impact India, particularly assistance to Pakistan's nuclear and missile programs.) Pakistan, in turn, perceives dangers in India's posture changes and make its own adjustments. Pakistani adjustments can then prompt new or reinforce earlier Indian actions.

This South Asia nuclear polygon dynamic suggests a need for discussions at least among China, India, and Pakistan to gain insights into the perceptions and interests of each and to look for opportunities to enhance stability. Yet, as Salmaan notes, China does not recognize the triangular relationship much less want to be part of it. As earlier described and as the United States has found, China also generally is resistant to transparency measures on military matters, which it views as a potential vulnerability. The June 2020 Galwan Valley border clash between China and India only makes it harder for them to come together, even if it increases the need. As ever, there also is no shortage of obstacles to security dialogue between India and Pakistan.

Treaty on the Prohibition of Nuclear Weapons

In 2017, more than a year before the United States announced its intention to withdraw from the INF Treaty due to Russian noncompliance, a group of non-nuclear weapons states, already dissatisfied with the progress of nuclear-armed states to achieve nuclear disarmament, secured United Nations General Assembly approval to open for ratification a Treaty on the Prohibition of Nuclear Weapons (TPNW). The TPNW comprehensively prohibits nuclear weapons to each state party. Having achieved the requisite ratification by at least 50 states on 24 October 2020, the treaty will enter into force on 22 January 2021.[163]

For TPNW proponents, waiting on the nuclear weapons states to eliminate nuclear weapons pursuant to the NPT has been shown to be a false hope. Disarmament advocates heartened by U.S. President Barack Obama's commitment in his 2009 Prague Speech to work toward nuclear disarmament and conclusion the following year of the New START agreement with Russia subsequently would have been disillusioned by renewed tensions between the nuclear superpowers and the apparent retreat from arms control. TPNW proponents hope that a treaty that imposes positive obligations on states to disarm will ultimately achieve this goal. Entry into force alone, though, will not cause those non-signatories who possess nuclear weapons to give them up. Nuclear weapons states possess nuclear weapons to deter perceived threats to their most vital interests and do not view ratification as removing or sufficiently ameliorating those threats. TPNW proponents nonetheless look to the treaty to increase moral, political, and economic pressure upon nuclear weapons states that eventually will lead them to disarm.[164]

The TPNW is opposed by all states that possess nuclear weapons and U.S. allies who depend on the protection of the U.S. nuclear umbrella.[165] The United States considers the TPNW to be ineffective, unrealistic, and counterproductive, in part because it believes the proposed treaty will distract from and undermine nonproliferation efforts under the NPT and also because it could undermine extended deterrence.[166] Washington has advanced a competing multilateral initiative, Create the Environment for Nuclear Disarmament (CEND), which focuses on practical measures to reduce incentives for, and the risks associated with, nuclear weapons.[167] At the heart of the CEND effort is the conviction that real progress toward nuclear disarmament can only be achieved by addressing the security conditions underlying states' motivations to acquire and retain nuclear weapons. It has three lines of efforts concerning 1) incentives for countries to possess or eliminate nuclear weapons, 2) mechanisms to bolster and sustain nonproliferation and disarmament, and 3) how to manage and reduce nuclear risks until nuclear weapons are eliminated. As of September 2020, CEND involved the diplomatic participation of 43 countries, including states that have and have not supported the TPNW.[168] CEND's most important audience is U.S.-aligned democracies with significant anti-nuclear sentiment.

The TPNW reflects differences between the nuclear weapons "haves" (including non-nuclear weapons states that rely on the protection or stability afforded by extended nuclear deterrence) and "have nots" over the legitimacy of nuclear weapons and the utility of the current nuclear nonproliferation regime. These differences can adversely impact cooperation on specific measures to prevent proliferation, such as further restricting the availability of enrichment and reprocessing capabilities; adequately resourcing safeguards, monitoring and verification activities; and sanctioning violators. Disputes over aspirational matters already interfere with practical cooperation among NPT members states, such as when those member states did not issue a concluding statement at the 2015 Review Conference after failing to agree on language on a Middle East WMD Free Zone.[169] The environment may be even less conducive to practical cooperation when NPT states convene for the next Review Conference in 2021[170] absent positive developments regarding arms control and/or nuclear nonproliferation efforts regarding Iran and North Korea.

Implications for Nuclear Nonproliferation Going Forward

Prospects for halting and unwinding nuclear proliferation are less encouraging in 2020 than in 2014 or at some points in between. Despite pursuing at various times coercive and conciliatory approaches to ending nuclear weapons programs in North Korea and Iran, the United States has yet to achieve that purpose or looks close to doing so. Nuclear threats—one actualized and one potential—continue to hang over regional allies and partners of the United States in East Asia and the Middle East, and to generate concern that some of those allies and partners may end up pursuing their own nuclear weapons programs. At the same time, nuclear risks grow in South Asia. Disappointed by such developments as well as an apparent retreat by the nuclear superpowers from arms control and disarmament, many of the world's nuclear weapons "have nots" now are pursuing those ends through a quixotic new treaty to outlaw all nuclear weapons. This could possibly be at the expense of cooperation with the nuclear weapons "haves" under the NPT on more practical and incremental measures to reduce nuclear risks. By 2030, it is more likely that the number of nuclear weapons states, as well as the number of nuclear weapons, will have grown rather than diminished.

REGIMES UNDER PRESSURE: CHEMICAL AND BIOLOGICAL

The integrity of the Chemical Weapons Convention (CWC)[171] has come under further pressure in recent years by the employment of chemical weapons by several actors, most significantly Syria and Russia. The Biological and Toxin Weapons Convention (BWC)[172] has suffered no comparable violation, but the biological weapons nonproliferation regime is challenged to keep pace with burgeoning developments in the life sciences and enabling technologies. The coronavirus pandemic may have implications for biological threats going forward and the international communities' ability to respond to them.

CHEMICAL THREATS

The integrity of the CWC has been called into question since the 2014 paper as the result of chemical weapons use, especially by two CWC states parties, Syria and Russia, in direct violation of their CWC obligations. Other CWC states parties, led by the United States and its European allies, have worked together and in innovative ways to hold the violators to account and to deter future use but have had only limited success. Russia and Syria, working together and with the support of Iranian and Chinese partners, have opposed accountability efforts and managed to escape severe consequences. The two other actors that have used chemical weapons in recent years lie outside of the convention and are already heavily sanctioned (North Korea) or under attack (Islamic State) for other reasons. Any use of chemical weapons, even by actors not a party to the CWC, is an affront and corrosive to the international norm against the possession and employment of chemical weapons. As will be discussed later, how these four actors (Syria, Russia, North Korea, and Islamic State) used chemical weapons, for what purpose, and with what effect may also serve to motivate others to acquire and use such weapons and thereby compound challenges to the CWC.

Chemical Weapons Use in Armed Conflict

According to an analysis by the Global Public Policy Institute, by May 2020, chemical weapons had been used on at least 349 occasions over the course of the Syrian civil war, almost all of which are attributable to the Syrian regime of Bashar al-Assad.[173] Over 90 percent of the attacks attributed to the Syrian regime through 2018 involved the toxic industrial chemical chlorine; the rest involved the nerve agent sarin.[174] Unsurprisingly, given sarin's extreme lethality, the small number of sarin attacks caused by far the most deaths. The most lethal was the sarin attack in Eastern Ghouta in August 2013, resulting in approximately 1,400 fatalities.[175] The second most lethal attack, against Khan Shaykhun in April 2017, also involved sarin and caused approximately 100 deaths.[176] In contrast, more than 300 chlorine attacks resulted in about 200 deaths combined, although more than 5,000 other casualties have been linked to those attacks.[177] The most consequential chlorine attack took place in Douma in April 2018, involving about 50 deaths and hundreds wounded.[178]

The Global Public Policy Institute study found that chemical weapons have "proven a small but essential component of the Assad regime's war strategy, which revolves around campaigns of civilian punishment and displacement." Referring to this strategy as "collective punishment," the study observed, "Seeping into trenches, tunnels, and shelters, chemical agents complement the specific effects of conventional bombardment, leaving civilian populations no option but to leave opposition-held areas while depriving insurgents of popular legitimacy and resources."[179] The regime's chemical attacks were concentrated on soft civilian targets in rebel-held areas beyond the immediate front lines and exploited the populace's exceptional fear of chemical effects.[180] Though the number of chemical attacks was very small compared to conventional ones, they had outsized impact. A veteran member of a Syrian rebel group is quoted in the study as concluding, "The use of chemical weapons settled the equation in favor of the regime."[181]

Only the three most lethal attacks—Eastern Ghouta in 2013, Khan Shaykhun in 2017, and Douma in 2018—prompted actual or threatened international military action against the Syrian regime. Having earlier warned Syria that its movement or use of a "whole bunch of chemical weapons" would constitute a "red line" for the United States,[182] U.S. President Obama responded to the August 2013 sarin attack by threatening targeted military strikes against the Syrian regime.[183] He relented when the Syrian regime, under pressure from Russia, agreed to join the CWC. Syria formally acceded to the convention in September 2013, and, in accordance with its obligations, made a declaration of its chemical weapons program (including precursor chemicals, warheads, aerial bombs, production equipment, and storage sites) to the Organization for the Prohibition of Chemical Weapons (OPCW). The destruction of Syria's declared chemical weapons under international supervision was declared completed in January 2016.[184] As it turned out, however, Syria had not made a complete declaration of its chemical weapons program nor did it cease chemical weapons-related activities. Reports of renewed Syrian (chlorine) chemical attacks emerged in the first part of 2014. Indeed, approximately 90 percent of Syria's use of chlorine weapons would occur after the 2013 sarin attack.[185] At President Trump's direction, the United States conducted missile strikes against Syria within days of both the April 2017 sarin and April 2018 chlorine attacks. The response to the April 2018 attacks was executed jointly with France and the United Kingdom.[186]

With the exception of those two military strikes against the Syrian regime (and other strikes against Islamic State chemical capabilities in the context of the international community's broader war against that violent extremist organization), the United States and larger international community's response to Syria's more than 300 chemical weapons attacks has been diplomatic and economic. They have focused on documenting and attributing chemical attacks to hold Syria accountable and to deter future attacks, not just by the Syrian regime but by others, anywhere. The United States and EU also have sanctioned culpable Syrian individuals and entities for a range of sanctionable behavior, including committing mass atrocities.[187]

It has been difficult to ascertain and attribute chemical weapons attacks to the exacting standards of international organizations whose membership includes states allied or sympathetic to Syria.[188] International inspectors have needed to build technical cases so strong that they could not be dismissed by biased actors and would support effective action against those responsible. Syrian authorities and an unstable security environment often delayed—or in some cases denied—access by international inspectors to suspected chemical weapons use locations and witnesses. Chlorine also is hard to detect after the fact as it dissipates quickly in the environment.[189] The situation furthermore was unprecedented: repeated and continuing chemical weapons use by a state initially outside and then inside the CWC.

Nonetheless, the United States and like-minded OPCW members adapted to the situation and achieved a measure of success. In 2014, the OPCW established two teams to investigate Syrian actions. First, the Declaration Assessment Team (DAT) addressed questions about Syria's declaration of its chemical weapons program. The DAT made numerous visits to Syria, met with Syrian authorities, visited chemical weapons sites, and took samples for further evaluation. Meanwhile, the Fact-Finding Mission (FFM) collected information on alleged uses of chemical weapons in Syria, though with no mandate to determine responsibility. The FFM recorded many potential incidents (e.g., 65 just from December 2015 to November 2016), and reported as of 1 March 2019 that toxic chemicals were used or likely used in more than 30 incidents at 11 different locations, including chlorine at seven, sarin at three, and sulfur mustard at two.[190]

Since determining an attack likely occurred was necessary but not sufficient to hold perpetrators accountable, a Joint United Nations-OPCW Investigative Mechanism (JIM) was established pursuant to UNSC Resolution 2235 in 2015 to determine if any cases investigated by the FFM could be attributed. During its one-year mandate, the JIM determined that the Syrian regime was responsible for one sarin and three chlorine attacks, and additionally attributed three sulfur mustard attacks to Islamic State. The JIM expired in November 2017 after Russia blocked renewal of its mandate in the UNSC. In 2018, however, a special session of the CWC's Conference of States Parties (CSP) established by majority vote (and over the dissenting vote of Russia)[191] the Investigation and Identification Team (IIT). The IIT was commissioned to determine responsibility for attacks that the FFM had determined involved the use or likely use of chemical weapons in Syria and on which the JIM had not reached a final conclusion.[192] In its first report, issued in April 2020, the ITT concluded that there were reasonable grounds to believe that the Syrian regime had conducted a sarin attack in southern Ltamenah on 24 March 2017 and again on 30 March, and a chlorine attack on the Ltamenah hospital on 25 March.[193] The OPCW continues to pursue the Syrian case in an effort to hold the regime accountable.[194]

Beyond the OPCW and the United Nations, France founded the International Partnership Against Impunity for the Use of Chemical Weapons on 23 January 2018. This intergovernmental initiative brings together 40 states (including the United States, but not Russia or China) and the European Union "to supplement the international mechanisms to combat the proliferation of chemical weapons. It deals exclusively with the issue of impunity for the perpetrators of chemical attacks worldwide, and is a forum for cooperation among participating governments."[195] In a format similar to the multilateral Proliferation Security Initiative,[196] members ascribe to a "declaration of principles" and conduct regular meetings of experts.

Throughout the Syrian conflict, the Assad regime and its Russian and Iranian allies, with support from China, endeavored to shield the regime from culpability and consequence for its use of chemical weapons. As described in the reports of the international inspectors, Syria consistently delayed or in some cases denied access and information to international inspectors or failed to provide adequate security for those inspectors in the conduct of their investigations. Syria and Russia also consistently denied their responsibility for chemical attacks in Syria and blamed rebel forces without providing supporting evidence (an exception was Islamic State's use of sulfur mustard in Um-Housh in September 2016[197]). The Syrian regime additionally alleged numerous rebel chemical attacks that the FFM investigated but could not verify.[198] Russia, Iran, and China obstructed and narrowed the scope of investigative efforts at the OPCW or UNSC.[199]

Russia also is understood to be the principal purveyor of disinformation through social and other public media about Syrian chemical attacks. An analysis of disinformation efforts following the 7 April 2018 chemical attack in Douma found that synthetic online actors, i.e., bots, primarily utilized several thematic tactics, including efforts to "defame Western institutions in order to discredit their claims about Syrian use of chemical weapons; suggest jihadist responsibility for the attacks; hint that a destructive (often nuclear) escalation would result from a Western retaliatory strike; and to prey on Western religious and cultural sympathies for supposedly besieged Christians and the secular Bashar al-Assad regime."[200] Disinformation also can undermine confidence in the OPCW generally.

Chemical Weapons Use for Assassination

In 2018, Russia became more than a defender of Syria's perpetration of chemical attacks; it was exposed as conducting its own. On 4 March 2018—a year after the North Korean regime had used VX to assassinate Kim Jong Un's half-brother in Malaysia[201]—two Russian agents employed a "novichok" nerve agent in an attempt to assassinate a former Russian military intelligence officer, Sergei Skripal, where he lived in Salisbury, UK. Novichok is a class of chemical warfare agents developed by the Soviet Union during the Cold War that was not widely known nor listed on the CWC Schedules of Chemicals at the time of attack.[202] Skripal and his daughter, Yulia Skripal, were seriously injured, and a police detective also became ill from exposure to the agent.[203] Three months after the Salisbury attack, a man from Amesbury, UK, who had unwittingly found the discarded perfume bottle that the Russian agents used to dispense the agent, gave the dispenser to his partner, who applied the contents and died.[204]

Notwithstanding Russian denials of involvement and an active disinformation campaign that would continue for months after,[205] the UK uncovered and publicized compelling evidence of Russia's responsibility. Before the end of March 2018, more than 20 western countries, in a coordinated response, condemned Russia for the novichok attack and expelled over 100 Russian diplomats (60 by the United States).[206] The next month, the OPCW's Technical Secretariat publicly confirmed the UK's finding of the agent that had been used but did not attribute the attack.[207] The United States later imposed additional sanctions on Russia as mandated by the Chemical and Biological Weapons Control and Warfare Elimination Act.[208]

In October 2018, Canada, the Netherlands, and the United States moved to add two families of novichok agents to the CWC's Schedule of Chemicals, which had never been amended. The Russians countered with their own, longer list of chemicals to add, including novichoks as well as a different class of nerve agents (carbamates) that the United States had investigated but abandoned decades before. In November 2019, the Conference of States Parties approved the Western group's list and a modified version of the original Russian one, resulting in the addition of two families of novichoks, two of carbamates, and another, single novichok.[209]

Then, on 20 August 2020, Russia apparently again used a novichok-type of agent in an attempted assassination, this time against Alexei Navalny, the most prominent figure of the Russian opposition to the Putin regime. Navalny fell ill during a flight within Russia and eventually was allowed to be evacuated to Germany, where he was treated at a Berlin hospital. On 2 September 2020, the German government announced that Navalny's illness was caused by a chemical agent from the novichok group.[210] G7 foreign ministers shortly thereafter called upon Russia to provide transparency on who is responsible for the attack, though that is unlikely as Russia disavows any involvement.[211] On 6 October 2020, the OPCW confirmed that Navalny had been exposed to a novichok-type agent.[212] On 15 October 2020, the European Union imposed sanctions on six senior Russian officials and a Russian research institute.[213] Russia's action expresses deep disdain for the OPCW and can be expected to further undermine the norm against chemical weapons use.

Assessing the International Response to Chemical Weapons Use

The foregoing demonstrates that the CWC, OPCW, and the states committed to prohibiting chemical weapons proliferation and use have never been so challenged as in recent years, but they have adapted and innovated to remain relevant. Existing authorities have been more fully utilized to overcome an inability to achieve consensus among key players with divergent interests, and new mechanisms have been established and exercised to ascertain and attribute chemical weapons use. Official bodies benefited from the investigations and reporting of nongovernmental organizations, and all took advantage of far greater real- or near-real- time, on-the-ground information shared via social media.[214] Shaming, sanctions, and, in a few cases, military force have been applied to punish perpetrators and in an effort to deter future use.

Against these achievements in the cause of prohibiting chemical weapons proliferation and use must be weighed what the perpetrators achieved and avoided with their chemical attacks. Despite the actions of the OPCW, United Nations, and a number of individual nations, the Syrian regime, as U.S. Secretary of State Michael Pompeo observed in April 2020, "has repeatedly used chemical weapons every year since [acceding to the CWC in 2013] to retain its grip on power."[215] Moreover, the Syrian regime used chemical weapons as an integral part of a brutal but winning military strategy. In the case of Russia's use of novichok, Western states' rapid and coordinated response may have surprised and stung Moscow,[216] but did not appreciably add to Russia's political and economic burdens resulting from its actions in Ukraine. Indeed, three months after the Skripal incident, President Trump called for Russia to rejoin the G7 group, from which it had been suspended in 2014.[217] As a 2019 report on recent chemical weapons use and response by the Center for Strategic and International Studies found, "Syria and Russia have not met significant consequence for their continued violation of the [CWC] treaty from within the institution, a highly corrosive outcome for these norms and their restraining value."[218]

On balance, more actors today than a decade ago may judge chemical weapons to be a useful, and most likely covert, part of their arsenal, which can be employed with greater effect than cost under certain circumstances. Such circumstances, which differ from the large-scale, state-on-state battlefield use that occurred in World War I and a few instances since, will be considered next.

Implications for Chemical Weapons and Internal Control

Syria may not have originally acquired chemical weapons to use against its own citizens. The regime of Hafez al-Assad, father of the current Syrian president, is believed to have initiated Syria's chemical weapons program in the late 1970s as a strategic deterrent against external foes, especially an Israel thought to possess nuclear weapons.[219] But when civil war convulsed Syria in the past decade, chemical weapons were an instrument at hand for an embattled regime.

Bashar al-Assad also is not the first state leader to employ chemical weapons against his own citizens. For example, Saddam Hussein used chemical weapons during his 1988 Al-Anfal campaign against disaffected Kurdish Iraqis, and against Shiite countrymen in 1991.[220] Yet, the drafters of the CWC were more focused on chemical weapons as a state-to-state, large-scale battlefield threat than as a means of internal control. Gregory Koblentz has persuasively argued that regime security is an important but neglected explanation for why some authoritarian regimes seek and use chemical weapons.[221]

Bashar al-Assad, however, is the only state leader to use chemical weapons—systematically and over a period of years—against his own people since the CWC came into force. That he did so as an integral part of a winning military strategy and has endured all that the international community has thrown at him may motivate some other actors to give more consideration to chemical weapons for internal control. A lesson that other regimes are likely to draw from the Syrian experience is that low-lethal applications can have outsized benefits without provoking strong international responses, particular military ones. They also may note that having the support of a major power can blunt international responses and help ensure that they are bearable.[222] However, each regime's cost/benefit calculus of chemical weapons use will be situationally dependent. Having an external benefactor may have been a significant consideration for the Assad regime, but it presumably would be less so for a regime more capable of deterring external intervention on its own, such as North Korea.

Implications for Chemical Weapons and Gray Zone Conflict

Characteristics of some chemical weapons that proved useful to the Syrian regime for waging a civil conflict also could appeal to other states for external competition in the "gray zone." Inter-state competition below the level of armed conflict, sometimes also referred to as operating in the gray zone, is expected to be an increasingly important aspect of the future international security environment, figuring in the United

States' competition with great power rivals as well as rogue states.[223] In the gray zone, antagonists utilize a number of instruments in a variety of ways to seek advantage without provoking open, armed conflict. Some instruments are non-kinetic, such as information operations, cyber operations, and forms of economic warfare, while others may be kinetic but wielded in restrained or non-attributable ways intended not to cross an adversary's perceived threshold for initiating open, armed conflict.[224]

The use of some chemical and biological weapons may be hard to attribute or be of sufficiently low lethality so as not to provoke an adversary to escalate to a more lethal response. Syria's employment of chlorine demonstrated both traits. Attribution was difficult and time-consuming, and complicated by the efforts of Syria and its Russian ally to obstruct attribution efforts. Even when there was little doubt that Syria had employed the weapons, low-lethal incidents did not provoke Western states to military retaliation. Rebecca Hersman, Suzanne Claeys, and Cyrus Jabbari have used the analogy of a serial killer to describe Syria's actions, in that repeated, small-scale attacks over time attract less attention and are harder to attribute than the singular, large-scale, and dramatic action of a mass murderer.[225]

More technologically advanced states, like Russia, China, and Iran, likely could produce a wider selection of chemical and biological weapons specifically tailored for use in the gray zone, including low-lethal pharmaceutical-based agents (PBAs) and unrecognized novel agents. With regard to the former, the United States has publicly expressed its concern that Russia's PBA program is for offensive purposes and that Iran also may be pursuing PBAs to such ends.[226] As discussed in the 2014 paper, Russia had utilized aerosolized PBAs—two analogues of the synthetic opioid, fentanyl—to resolve a hostage crisis at a Moscow theater in 2002.[227] The Russian case demonstrated that fentanyl analogues intended to incapacitate can also be lethal, as approximately 130 of 850 hostages exposed to the fentanyl died. That some PBAs are too dangerous for the standards of law enforcement is the principal reason why Australia, Switzerland, and the United States are leading an effort within the OPCW to recognize that the aerosolized use of central nervous-system acting chemicals (CNSAC), a subset of PBAs, is inconsistent with law enforcement purposes as a "purpose not prohibited" under the Convention.[228] Another reason pertinent to conflict in the gray zone is that allowing agents with such a wide range of effects to be possessed and used for law enforcement would also provide cover for disingenuous CWC state parties to ready those chemicals for military use.[229]

There also are known viruses and bacteria that can be more disabling than lethal for most people, as well as those currently unknown that may emerge in the future from nature or as the product of biotechnology. Pathogens currently unknown will be particularly hard to identify, distinguish from naturally occurring disease, counter, and attribute, which should appeal to unlawful actors prosecuting conflict in the gray zone. Attribution also would require disease surveillance activities that may be difficult or impossible to conduct in a conflict zone.

Disinformation operations can and have been used to reinforce or complement physical characteristics of chemicals and biological organisms that help to obscure their identity and origin. Countries are particularly sensitive to allegations that they have used WMD, so it is unsurprising that such allegations have been prominent targets of recent disinformation operations. As previously discussed, Moscow used disinformation to discredit allegations of Syria's and its own chemical weapons use. Beijing has used disinformation to deflect attention from its role in the coronavirus pandemic and has benefited from amplification of its narratives by Iran and Russia.[230] Some U.S. political figures have suggested that the novel coronavirus escaped from a Chinese laboratory and have been criticized for doing so without sufficient supporting evidence.[231]

Disinformation operations have multiple audiences and can be successful if they favorably affect perceptions in only some of them, whether by persuading target audiences that a particular narrative is true or by generating so many competing narratives that it is impossible to determine what occurred.[232] Russian and Chinese disinformation operations may have done little to persuade Americans that Russia was not responsible for the employment of novichok and that China was not negligent in its initial response to its coronavirus outbreak, but they were persuasive to their own populations.[233] Sophisticated disinformation campaigns also can provide cover to other actors for their diplomatic support, especially when those other actors were predisposed for their own interests to be supportive.[234] Disinformation, already prevalent among gray zone tactics, can be expected to be an important component of future use of chemical and biological weapons. Together, they can be viewed as complementary pieces of multi-domain operations.

Implications for Chemical Weapons Use by Non-State Actors

Islamic State, a jihadist violent extremist group,[235] also repeatedly used chemical weapons in Syria, as well as in Iraq, during 2015-2017. Islamic State exploited the relative security and significant resources, including industrial and scientific, of the so-called caliphate to employ toxic industrial chemicals, like chlorine; low-quality sulfur mustard; and improvised delivery vehicles. Ironically, for a terrorist organization, Islamic State predominantly used chemical weapons in a more traditional manner, directing them mainly against opposing forces, than did state actors Syria and Russia.[236] Islamic State fared less well than the Syrian regime, as its use of chemical and other weapons did not enable it to hold onto the territory it had seized in Syria and Iraq. However, it gained expertise and experience in chemical weapons that it may be able to wield in future operations. Its expertise and experience also may find its way to other non-state actors, particularly jihadist ones, including through Islamic State's extensive online presence.[237]

BIOLOGICAL THREATS

Biological Weapons

Since 2014, the BWC has suffered no apparent violations comparable to those experienced by the CWC. No country is known to have employed biological weapons, nor are any terrorist groups known to have mounted biological attacks, despite periodic claims to the contrary. Nevertheless, BWC proponents worry that the biological weapons nonproliferation regime also is at risk.

The United States government has expressed concerns that at least four countries—China, Iran, North Korea, and Russia—may not be in compliance with their obligations under the provisions of the BWC.[238]

In 2017, the Joint Chiefs of Staff went further and informed Congress that it feared that "North Korea may consider the use of biological weapons."[239] As noted in the 2014 paper, Putin had called for the creation of what were termed "genetic" weapons. While it is not specifically known what this meant, this and related activity led some analysts to suspect that the Russian government might be attempting to reenergize the former Soviet biological weapons program.[240] Compliance concerns, however, have existed since the late 1970s without seriously undermining the norm, so there is no necessary reason to expect significant additional erosion of the norm resulting from these recent compliance concerns.

Others worry about possible diminishing international support for the biological arms control regime. The regular BWC meetings, especially the Meetings of States Parties, have become increasingly contentious. The Iranians continue to promote a failed 1990s attempt to augment the BWC with a verification protocol that the United States believed would have undermined the convention.[241] To further that objective, the Iranians have obstructed other efforts to strengthen the BWC. The BWC is further hampered by limited funding, exacerbated by the failure of some countries to pay their dues on time. As a result, meetings have had to be curtailed, and it has not been possible to expand the treaty's Implementation Support Unit beyond its current staff of only three people. Finally, there is growing concern that rapid advances in the biological sciences are outpacing the ability to evaluate or mitigate their security implications. This concern has been accentuated for some by the absence of a standing scientific advisory board comparable to the one that supports the OPCW on chemical weapons issues.[242]

Another concern about the regime arises from the growing willingness of some countries to make allegations of biological weapons in propaganda campaigns. Since 2011, Russian government officials have repeatedly claimed that the United States has either acquired or employed biological agents in violation of the BWC, reviving a disinformation campaign from the Soviet era. Thus, it has claimed that the biological laboratories built in the Republic of Georgia and other countries are components of an active U.S. biological weapons program.[243] Even more seriously, the Russians alleged that the laboratory in the Republic of Georgia was responsible for the deliberate introduction of African swine fever (ASF) into Russia.[244] More recently, Chinese, Iranian, and Russian sources have asserted that the United States was responsible for the COVID-19 pandemic.[245] These claims extend a long history of bioweapons-oriented disinformation efforts that began in the Soviet Union and had the goal of fostering anti-American sentiment abroad, favorable sentiment toward the Soviet Union and its allies, and political controversy in the United States.[246] Such groundless allegations threaten to spread the belief that biological weapons are used widely, implying that the BWC is not preventing biological warfare. None of the countries making these accusations has made use of the measures to address such violations that are provided in international agreements.

COVID-19

Some counterterrorism experts fear that the coronavirus (COVID-19) pandemic will increase the prospects for bioterrorism. That advances in the biological science could make it easier for terrorist groups to acquire and employ biological weapons is not a new observation. As noted elsewhere, the pandemic has demonstrated the vulnerability of modern societies to large-scale disease outbreak, which at least some counterterrorism experts believe might raise the perceived attractiveness of bioterrorism. In the words of one former counterterrorism official, "The severity and extreme disruption of a novel coronavirus will likely spur the imagination of the most creative and dangerous groups and individuals to reconsider bio-terrorist attacks."[247]

While it is too soon to estimate the broader impact of the COVID-19 pandemic on the international system or its specific implications for WMD, at least one observation can be made: The resulting geopolitical disruptions illustrate the fragility of the existing international order, raising concerns that earlier patterns of collaboration and cooperation may not be the norm in future crises. Efforts to develop an international pandemic response architecture have been slow and insufficient. Countries competed to acquire critical medical supplies, such as personal protective equipment. China did not join the WHO-led effort to coordinate international coronavirus vaccine efforts until October 2020, and the United States remained outside the effort, as of this writing. The COVID-19 experience has brought into starker relief the U.S. step back from global leadership that predated the pandemic, likely resulting in a slower and less robust pandemic response.

EXPANDING USE OF FINANCIAL SANCTIONS

U.S. financial sanctions are among the most powerful non-military instruments of U.S. policy, including against WMD proliferation. U.S. financial sanctions played an important role in bringing Iran to negotiations over its nuclear program and its agreeing to the JCPOA. The re-imposition of sanctions since the United States withdrew from the agreement is again inflicting pain on Iran's economy and regime. U.S. financial measures also are part of the economic sanctions imposed on North Korea for its nuclear program. Relief from those sanctions is that regime's principal demand for any denuclearization concessions. On 20 August 2020, the United States explicitly marked the seventh anniversary of the chemical attack in eastern Ghouta by imposing additional sanctions on members of the Syrian regime.[248] As David Cohen said in 2014, while Under Secretary of the Treasury for Terrorism and Financial Intelligence, "Financial power has become an essential component of our country's national-security toolkit. That fact may mean that we are called on to use it more frequently and in more complex ways than we have in previous decades."[249] Over time, however, over-reliance on U.S. financial sanctions may undermine their power along with the United States' dominant position within the international financial system.

Expanding Use

The United States began to use financial sanctions in 2001 to cut off funding for terrorism and increasingly has turned to this instrument in the years since.[250] Also sometimes known as smart, list-based, or targeted sanctions, financial sanctions differ from an earlier type of economic sanctions by restricting the access of specific individuals or entities to the U.S. financial system rather than broadly prohibiting trade with a country. Those earlier, country-based economic sanctions were blunt instruments, affecting a country's population generally and hard to police. An even more recent type of sanction, known as "secondary sanctions," applies to third parties that engage in prohibited economic activity with the targeted actor, significantly extending the reach of the financial sanctions regime and reducing the targeted actor's ability to evade it.[251]

As David Cohen went on to explain in his December 2014 remarks, financial sanctions work for several reasons. Because of "the preeminence of U.S. capital markets and the dollar's dominant role in global trade…financial institutions everywhere need dollars to serve their customers, and thus require access to U.S. banks through correspondent accounts to settle their customers' transactions." The "transparent, well-regulated" nature of the financial system and the U.S. Treasury's ability to combine the expertise, functions, and technology of a finance ministry and intelligence agency enable the United States to exploit its dominant position to identify specific illicit actors and deny them access.[252] An academic expert summarizes the situation: "The United States has successfully weaponized its unique economic and financial capabilities and is able to impose punishing sanctions that disrupt access of opponents and their supporters through America's proprietary nodes to the global banking system."[253]

U.S. financial sanctions are used to combat a broad range of illicit activities in addition to WMD proliferation, including terrorism, narcotics trafficking, human rights abuses, and other threats to national security.[254] Treasury is the lead department for U.S. financial sanctions efforts, and its responsible organization is the Office of Terrorism and Financial Intelligence (TFI). TFI has two components: the Office of Terrorist Financing and Financial Crimes, which handles policy and outreach, and the Office of Intelligence and Analysis, which handles intelligence functions and integrates Treasury into the larger U.S. Intelligence Community. TFI also oversees the Office of Foreign Assets Control (OFAC), which administers and enforces economic and trade sanctions; Treasury's Executive Office for Asset Forfeiture, which administers the receipt account for the deposit of non-tax forfeitures; and Financial Crimes Enforcement Network (FinCEN), which supports law enforcement investigative efforts and fosters interagency and global cooperation against domestic and international financial crimes.[255] FinCEN works with the International Financial Action Task Force (FATF), a body currently composed of 37 countries and two regional organizations, which sets global standards and evaluates compliance with anti-money-laundering efforts.[256] TFI also has arrangements with the Society for Worldwide Interbank Financial Telecommunication (SWIFT), a cooperative of major international banks and other financial institutions that forms the communications backbone of the formal international financial system, providing essential insight on certain aspects of international financial transactions.[257]

Financial sanctions became an instrument for countering WMD proliferation in June 2005, when President George W. Bush signed Executive Order (EO) 13382. That EO authorizes the U.S. Treasury Secretary to identify and freeze the assets of anyone involved in or facilitating WMD proliferation as well as any entities owned or controlled by those involved.[258] OFAC implements the sanctions program established by E.O. 13382, as well as the Weapons of Mass Destruction Trade Control Regulations (31 C.F.R., Part 539), which implement a ban on imports into the United States from those determined to have engaged in proliferation-related activities; and the Highly Enriched Uranium (HEU) Agreement Assets Control Regulations (31 C.F.R, Part 540), directed at property used to carry out U.S.-Russian agreements for the conversion of HEU.[259] In the same timeframe that E.O. 13382 was signed, TFI initiated an effort at the FATF to make proliferation financing a focus of the world's leading anti-money-laundering body. The resulting standards were formally adopted by FATF in 2012 as part of the International Standards on Combating Money Laundering and the Financing of Terrorism and Proliferation.[260]

The Obama administration expanded the use of financial sanctions, including secondary sanctions. Most notably, it applied them successfully to pressure Iran to negotiate over its nuclear program and as part of a less fruitful effort to induce Russia to end its intervention in Ukraine. The Trump administration has used sanctions even more extensively. In its January 2020 report on economic sanctions, the Gibson Dunn law firm reported that the Trump administration added names to OFAC's Specially Designated Nationals and Blocked Persons (SDN) List at more than twice the average annual increase seen under the two previous administrations.[261] U.S. citizens and residents are prohibited from doing business with foreign nationals and organizations that appear on the SDN.[262] At the same time, the Trump administration has made unprecedented use of tariff authorities, including invoking a rarely-used national security provision to impose levies on the goods of U.S. allies.[263]

Implications of Expanded Use

Other states, including great power rivals, have benefited from the transparency, liquidity, and rules-based nature of the U.S.-dominated international financial system, but they are wary of the power it confers upon the United States. Their wariness is tempered when the United States exercises that power to advance a widely shared goal, such as cutting off funding for terrorism and moving Iran to negotiate over its nuclear program. It is heightened when U.S. sanctions are used to advance a contentious goal or directly against their own interests.[264]

The re-imposition of U.S. sanctions against Iran after the United States unilaterally withdrew from the JCPOA offended other influential countries on both counts: the other JCPOA parties opposed the United States' withdrawal as a matter of policy, and U.S. secondary sanctions disadvantaged their own entities engaged, or seeking to engage, in JCPOA-permitted commerce with Iran. Iran is the largest state target of U.S. sanctions.[265] Some European states also oppose U.S. unilateral sanctions against entities involved in a German-Russian project to build a pipeline to carry Russian energy resources across the Baltic Sea to Europe, even while supporting other U.S. sanctions aimed at Russia for its intervention in Ukraine. European states may further resent that their banks incurred the bulk of the value of penalties assessed by the United States since 2008 for sanctions violations. China also has been increasingly targeted by sanctions as well as tariffs to penalize it for unfair economic practices.[266]

The perceived abuse of U.S. financial sanctions is motivating other states to pursue workarounds to the U.S.-dominated financial system. Since 2013, Russia has reduced the value of U.S. dollar-denominated assets among its international currency reserves from 40 percent to 24 percent.[267] In 2018, the European Union updated its EU Blocking Statute—originally passed in 1996 to protect EU operators from the extra-territorial application of certain U.S. sanctions—to cover the United States' re-imposition of sanctions pursuant to its JCPOA withdrawal.[268] In 2019, commercial entities, including some Iranian ones, were able to exploit the updated statute to secure enforcement of contracts impacted by U.S. sanctions through the national courts of EU states.[269] Also in 2019, France, Germany, and the UK launched the Instrument in Support of Trade Exchanges (INSTEX) to facilitate barter exchanges that would enable firms to conduct JCPOA-permitted trade with Iran without having to use U.S. dollars, though it has not yet had much success.[270]

China's efforts, however, may have the most potential over time to bypass or create alternatives to U.S.-dominated aspects of the international financial system.[271] As previously discussed, the U.S. dollar's status as the world's dominant reserve currency is what most fundamentally enables the power of U.S. financial sanctions. China has made clear its desire to establish its money, the renminbi (yuan), as a global reserve currency.[272] While it still has far to go, China has the growing economic heft as well as an expanding international trade and financial presence, especially among emerging economies, to make a go of it over time.[273] China also has an advantage over the EU in being a unitary actor.

In 2015, the International Monetary Fund (IMF) decided to include the yuan in the basket of currencies comprising its Special Drawing Rights (SDR) designation, along with the U.S. dollar, euro, yen, and British pound.[274] Since implementation of the IMF decision in 2016, the yuan's share of global reserves has risen every quarter, albeit only to 2.1% by September 2019.[275] China also has opened its $13 trillion bond market, which represents half of bonds issued by emerging economies; is easing its capital controls; and has established itself as a trusted debtor—all of which should increase demand for the yuan as a reserve currency.[276] China also is working on a sovereign digital currency and already has rolled out an alternative (known as CIPS) to SWIFT as a means for clearing international financial transactions.[277] Chinese firms additionally are leading the competition to provide the hardware and software that power banking payment systems.[278] Success in these endeavors would provide users with alternatives to the U.S. banking system.

Actions to diminish the role of the U.S. dollar, and, hence, the United States, in the international financial system have had only limited impact to date. The United States maintains huge advantages. Eighty percent of all global trade and more than 60 percent of central bank reserves are denominated in U.S. dollars.[279] Yet the United States courts trouble over time if the perceived abuse of financial sanctions continues to motivate powerful economic actors, particularly China and the European Union, to pursue ways to diminish the role of the U.S. dollar in international trade and finance.[280] Their efforts can reduce the power of the sanctions[281]—including to counter WMD proliferation[282]—and deprive the United States of the considerable economic advantages it derives from being the international financial system's pivot, such as reduced costs for financing its growing deficit spending.[283]

NEW DELIVERY VEHICLES

Delivery vehicles are an important aspect of the WMD challenge that largely were unaddressed in the 2014 paper. Recent developments of significance regarding delivery vehicles include the end of the INF Treaty, the emergence of new hypersonic systems, adversary efforts to develop nuclear-powered strike systems, further development and proliferation of unmanned systems, and continuing advances in precision guidance and remote sensing capabilities. These developments increase the reach, tempo, and effectiveness of systems that can profoundly affect strategic and operational environments, whether by delivering WMD or conventional payloads.

THE END OF THE INF TREATY

The INF Treaty's demise ended the international legal constraint upon the United States' and Russia's testing and deployment of ground-launched, medium- and intermediate-range ballistic and cruise missiles.[284] Established in the waning years of the Cold War to remove a threat posed mainly by European-based nuclear-armed missiles to strategic targets in the Soviet Union and Western Europe, the INF Treaty became increasingly anachronistic as the Soviet Union gave way to Russia, China overtook Russia as the world's second power, and missile and missile defense technology advanced.

Russia expressed frustration with INF Treaty constraints years before it was discovered to have tested the 9M729 ground-launched cruise missile (since deployed) in violation of those constraints, the material breach that the United States cited in announcing its withdrawal from the agreement on 2 February 2019.[285] Putin felt disadvantaged because other countries besides the United States were not similarly constrained, and the United States enjoyed an advantage in air- and sea-launched cruise missiles, which were not banned by the treaty.[286] Ground-based missiles are less expensive than the platforms on which air- or sea-launched ones are deployed. They also are particularly well suited to a continent-sized country like Russia, which perceives threats along much of its periphery. Countries along that periphery, including China, Iran, and North Korea, are developing and have fielded INF-range missiles.[287]

Russia evidently preferred to covertly develop a missile system in violation of the treaty than to withdraw from that agreement. It was to Moscow's advantage that the United States remain compliant and for Russia to avoid the political costs of abrogating the treaty. But it would have become increasingly apparent to Moscow beginning in the mid-2010s that the gambit was not going to work as the United States discovered and pursued the 9M729 violation with Moscow. That Russia persevered suggests it felt it had more to gain from doing so than from returning to compliance.

As it became clear that Russia would not acknowledge, much less make amends for, its improper testing of the 9M729, the United States initiated treaty-compliant research and development (short of flight testing) of INF-range missiles in 2017. The United States may have hoped that preparing for the treaty's possible demise would lead Russia to return to compliance, similar to how the United States and NATO's decision to develop and field the Pershing II ballistic missile and BGM-109G cruise missile induced the Soviet Union to negotiate and agree on the INF Treaty. Yet the United States' treaty-compliant research and development also had the effect of laying groundwork for new missile systems useful for countering China, which already deploys over a thousand INF-range missiles.[288] Just after the effective date of its treaty withdrawal, the United States conducted its first test of a system the agreement would have proscribed.[289]

The United States has not indicated what ground-launched INF-range missiles it will deploy and where it will deploy them, but it does not plan to arm them with nuclear warheads.[290] This stands in contrast to China, which already fields nuclear- as well as conventionally armed INF-range missiles, and Russia, which is expected to field a nuclear-armed version of the 9M729.[291] As previously discussed, the United States has decided to field sea-based nuclear missiles (low-yield warheads on submarine-launched ballistic missiles, and, later, the sea-launched cruise missile) to respond to Russia's growing force of theater-range nuclear weapons.

The United States will develop and field conventionally armed, ground-launched INF-range missiles principally to counter China's and Russia's anti-access/area denial (A2/AD) capabilities.[292] As well as being more cost-effective than air- or sea-launched systems (especially if existing missiles systems, like Tomahawk and Joint Air-to-Surface Missile-Extended Range, are adapted as land-based missiles),[293] they can be emplaced in range of their targets during peacetime and always stand ready for employment. They also are more survivable than aircraft on the ground or ships in port if they are mobile and based in locations that afford large dispersal areas.[294]

The United States' ability to hold its great power competitors at risk with ground-based, INF-range missiles, however, will be heavily dependent on allies and partners' willingness to host them. The United States has no territory of its own in the European theater, and its territories in the Indo-Pacific theater are small, which makes missiles and other assets based there more vulnerable to Chinese strikes. The most suitable locations for missile survivability in the Indo-Pacific theater are Japan's more spacious Kyushu prefecture and Australia,[295] as well as the Philippines. However, initial indications from key allies in the Indo-Pacific theater suggest an unwillingness to host U.S. INF-range missile strike systems.[296] Regional allies do not want to provoke China, who has warned them not to play host.[297] The Philippines under President Duterte is especially unlikely to offend China by accommodating U.S. missile systems. In Europe, NATO has not directly addressed the possibility of deploying conventional INF-range missiles, while making clear that it has no intention of deploying new land-based nuclear missiles. Poland has said it is against hosting U.S. ground-launched, intermediate-range missiles, though without reference to the types of warheads.[298] Yet, aggressive Russian and Chinese behavior could make allies more amenable to hosting U.S. ground-launched, INF-range missile systems by the time they become available.

Russia has sought to forestall the deployment of U.S. ground-launched, INF-range missiles to Europe with a moratorium proposal. On the day that the U.S. treaty withdrawal took effect, Putin announced that Russia would not deploy INF-range missiles to certain areas unless the United States did and invited the United States and NATO also to declare a moratorium.[299] The following month, he formally conveyed the proposal in a letter to NATO, which also was shared with China and the European Union.[300] NATO quickly rejected the offer, indicating it was not credible as Russia already had deployed the 9M729 missile in western Russia.[301] France joined NATO's rejection of the Russian proposal, but French President Emmanuel Macron also said that NATO "shouldn't just brush it off" and suggested that Europeans need to be part of any future agreement.[302] China has not indicated any interest in being part of a moratorium.

Russia's moratorium proposal may be intended to shift responsibility to the United States for ending restraints on INF-range missiles, especially in the eyes of Europeans. Yet, it also likely reflects Russia's longstanding concern about the threat that U.S. ground-launched, INF-range missiles in Europe could pose to its strategic deterrent, especially nuclear command and control assets, given short flight times. That concern motivated the Soviet Union to agree to the INF Treaty in 1987, when the threat emanated from nuclear-armed missiles. As earlier discussed, Russia subsequently has evinced worry about the danger that could be posed to its strategic deterrent by the United States' pursuit of conventional prompt strike capabilities, given advances in precision guidance since the Cold War and missile defense. Thus, even U.S. conventionally armed, ground-launched, INF-range missiles concern the Russians, and that concern will heighten as the United States is able to deploy hypersonic missiles. The United States may be able to leverage this Russian concern to negotiate constraints on INF-range missiles in the European theater while preserving its flexibility to deploy such systems in the Indo-Pacific region, if it chooses to do so.[303]

HYPERSONIC MISSILES

Hypersonic weapons systems operate at speeds greater than Mach 5.[304] Traditional long-range ballistic missile reentry vehicles travel at hypersonic speeds as well but lack maneuverability following a ballistic trajectory. Traditional cruise missiles are maneuverable but travel below hypersonic speeds. The emerging class of hypersonic vehicles are both fast and maneuverable.[305] They include hypersonic boost-glide vehicles (HGVs), which are launched (boosted) by a rocket to an apogee and then descend into the atmosphere where they use aerodynamic forces to glide at hypersonic speed to their targets; and hypersonic cruise missiles (HCMs), which are launched from a rocket or aircraft with a small solid rocket motor to give them enough velocity for their advanced air-breathing engines (ramjet or scramjet) to kick in and propel them through the atmosphere at hypersonic speeds to their targets.[306] HGVs are similar to existing maneuvering reentry vehicles (MaRVs) for ballistic missiles to the extent they both exploit the ability to glide and maneuver in the atmosphere, but HGVs do so much earlier in their flight profile than MaRVs and with less predictability as to their target. HCMs could reach a target 1,000 kilometers away within 10 minutes as compared to an hour for the Tomahawk cruise missile.[307]

The speed, altitude, and maneuverability of HGVs and HCMs make them almost impossible to defeat with existing air and missile defenses. They can travel below the intercept range of current mid-course missile defenses, like AEGIS or THAAD, and above that of air and point missile defenses, like PATRIOT.[308] The United States is investing in a new space-based sensor layer to enable earlier tracking and more intercept opportunities of hypersonic missiles.[309] Other emerging capabilities, such as cannons or rail guns firing hypervelocity projectiles, directed energy weapons, and even space-based interceptors, may be part of future defenses against hypersonic missile systems.[310]

Hypersonic vehicles are only starting to become available.[311] HGVs are at the forefront, as HCMs must overcome greater engineering challenges.[312] Hypersonic vehicles also are expensive, which will limit their numbers.[313] Russia has flight tested *Avangard*, an HGV launched from a heavy ICBM (probably the *Sarmat*, when available).[314] It has a number of other hypersonic vehicles in development, including the *Tsirkon* anti-ship cruise missile and the *Kinzhal* air-launched, maneuverable ballistic missile.[315] China has deployed a ballistic missile with a MaRV that reportedly can target ships underway (DF-21D "carrier killer")[316] and has placed heavy emphasis on developing and testing hypersonic weapon systems. For example, in August 2018, it successfully tested the XINGKONG-2 (*Starry Sky-2*) HCM, which it publicly described as a hypersonic wave-rider vehicle. China also featured the DF-17 medium-range ballistic missile designed to launch an HGV[317] for the first time in its 70th anniversary parade in 2019.[318] The United States, an early leader in hypersonic technology, now is having to catch up with Russian and Chinese advances.[319] The U.S. Army, Navy, and Air Force are reported to be each developing HGVs, and the Defense Advanced Research Programs Agency (DARPA) is working on an HCM.[320] The Air Force also is reported to have requested information from industry regarding an HCM,[321] and the Army is looking at a Strategic Long-Range Cannon that could fire hypervelocity projectiles.[322] No U.S. hypersonic vehicle is expected to be ready for deployment before the mid-2020s.[323] The UK, France, India, Japan, and Australia also have acknowledged research and testing of hypersonic capabilities but are considered unlikely to be able to deploy operational systems until well after 2030.[324]

Conventionally armed hypersonic missile systems are likely to have a more significant impact on military competition and conflict than nuclear-armed ones. The United States currently has no plans to develop new nuclear-armed hypersonic missile systems, and Russia and China appear to be developing theirs first and foremost to ensure their ability to penetrate future U.S. missile defense systems.[325] While nuclear-armed hypersonic missile systems fired from platforms close to U.S. shores could strike critical elements of the U.S. strategic nuclear force, including the national command authority, within minutes, the same could be achieved by traditional, sea-launched ballistic missiles on depressed trajectories.[326] In either case, the U.S. force of underway ballistic missile submarines would all but ensure a devastating retaliatory strike.[327] Enabling a disarming first strike against the U.S. strategic nuclear force is not a sufficient explanation for Russia's and China's pursuit of new nuclear-armed hypersonic missile systems, but ensuring enough of their strategic ballistic missiles can penetrate future and presumably more capable U.S. missile defenses to deter a U.S. first strike is.[328]

Conventionally armed hypersonic missiles with precision guidance also have the potential to rapidly destroy or disable some particularly important elements of an adversary's critical military infrastructure, especially soft leadership targets, which directly bear on both nuclear and conventional forces. Such conventional strikes would not have as comprehensive an impact on strategic forces as nuclear strikes; for example, it would be prohibitively expensive for an attacker to build a force of conventionally armed hypersonic missiles big enough to destroy most of Russia's or the United States' large forces of silo-protected ICBMs. However, their disabling or disruptive impact would be achieved without crossing the nuclear threshold. The heavy burden of escalating to nuclear war would lie with the victim of such conventional strikes. Both the United States and Russia have enough concern about the potential strategic impact of non-nuclear strikes enabled by new technologies—including kinetic attacks by hypersonic missiles—that they recently clarified their declaratory policies to say they would consider nuclear responses to non-nuclear strategic attacks (U.S. terminology).[329]

As discussed above, the United States is interested in conventionally armed hypersonic missiles as a means to counter Chinese and Russian anti-access/area-denial (A2/AD) capabilities.[330] In the Indo-Pacific theater, China's heavy investment in ground-based medium- and intermediate-range missiles, many of them mobile, increasingly enables that country to strike approaching U.S. forces before they can range Chinese systems. This is making it progressively more dangerous for U.S. forces to operate within the first island chain.[331] Conventionally armed, precision-guided, INF-range hypersonic missiles, supported with superior intelligence, surveillance, and reconnaissance (ISR) capabilities, could provide U.S. forces with the speed and range to strike Chinese A2/AD systems, even mobile ones, before they can be fired.[332] In the European theater, such systems could blunt the reach of Russian strike and air-defense systems that make it dangerous for U.S. and NATO forces to operate in the Baltic and Barents Seas and difficult to flow reinforcements across the Atlantic and through Western Europe. Of course, China and Russia can be expected to field their own hypersonic missile systems to target these and other U.S. power projection capabilities, but the U.S. investment helps ensure that the approaches to their homelands—which include allies and other interests important to the United States—remain at least contestable, with an attendant deterrent effect on potential aggression.

NUCLEAR-PROPELLED STRIKE SYSTEMS

Russia is developing two nuclear-propelled, nuclear-armed strike systems, *Poseidon* and *Burevestnik*, that, if realized, could enable virtually unlimited range and direction of attack, though not likely with any significant impact on the strategic nuclear balance.

Poseidon (NATO designator: KANYON) is an unmanned underwater drone powered with a miniature nuclear reactor. In 2015, a slide detailing the system from a Russian Ministry of Defense (MoD) briefing that appeared in the press indicated that the drone could reach a depth of 1,000 meters, go at the speed of 100 knots, and have a range of up to 10,000 kilometers. It is designed to "destroy important economic installations of the enemy in coastal areas and cause guaranteed devastating damage to the country's territory by creating wide areas of radioactive contamination, rendering them unusable for military, economic or other activity for a long time."[333] In 2018, Putin described *Poseidon* as able to "move at great depths (I would say extreme depths) intercontinentally, at a speed multiple times higher than the speed of submarines, cutting-edge torpedoes and all kinds of surface vessels, including some of the fastest."[334] The drone would be armed with a nuclear warhead, estimates of whose yield range from several megatons to 450 kilotons.[335] There are believed to be plans to deploy 32 *Poseidon* drones on four submarines, two in the Northern Fleet and two in the Pacific Fleet. Russia reportedly has been testing *Poseidon* since 2016 but may not deploy the system until 2027.[336]

Burevestnik (NATO designator: SKYFALL) is a cruise missile powered by a miniature nuclear reactor. Putin characterized the system as a "low-flying stealth cruise missile carrying a nuclear warhead, with almost an unlimited range, unpredictable trajectory and ability to bypass interception boundaries. . . . It is invincible against all existing and projected missile defense and counter-air defense systems." He described the miniature nuclear reactor as "a small-scale heavy-duty nuclear energy unit that can be installed in a missile like our latest X-101 air-launched missile or the American Tomahawk missile."[337] Russia reportedly has been conducting tests with a prototype and an electric (vice nuclear) power source since 2016, with most of the tests having failed. In August 2019, the nuclear reactor of a *Burevestnik* missile exploded off the coast of a northern Russian town, killing a number of Russians overseeing the recovery of the sunken missile and causing a radiation leak.[338] Some reports indicate that Russia is unlikely to be able to deploy the cruise missile for at least a decade.[339]

The concept of nuclear-propelled strike systems is not new. The United States initiated a program in the early 1960s, Project Pluto, to develop a nuclear reactor for a nuclear-armed cruise missile. The project was cancelled in 1964 shortly after a successful static test of its nuclear engine, largely due to fear of how dangerous a flying nuclear reactor could be in peacetime. In the same timeframe, Russian physicist Andrei Sakharov, as indicated in his memoirs, suggested to a Soviet admiral the development of an underwater system similar to *Poseidon*, but the admiral reacted with disgust and Sakharov never raised the concept again.[340]

Like nuclear-armed hypersonic missiles, it is not evident that nuclear-propelled, nuclear-armed strike systems like *Poseidon* and *Burevestnik* would significantly impact the strategic nuclear balance. They would, however, reinforce Russia's ability to penetrate U.S. missile defenses. They could add another element to Russia's nuclear first-strike capacity but should not deny the United States' ability to conduct a massive retaliatory strike, at least while the U.S. sea-based strategic deterrent remains secure. If armed with a conventional warhead, though there is no indication that is Russia's intention, *Burevestnik* could provide an exceptionally ready and flexible means to strike high-value targets given its endurance, but hypersonic missiles would probably be a cheaper and certainly less dangerous means to that end. It is hard to imagine that a conventionally armed *Poseidon* would offer any advantage over traditional torpedoes and unmanned underwater vehicles that could justify its greater cost. Some experts have expressed skepticism that these development programs will succeed, particularly that for *Burevestnik*, and speculate that Moscow may be highlighting them to shape perceptions of Russian technological sophistication and strength rather than relying upon them to fill operational roles.[341]

UNMANNED SYSTEMS

Unmanned systems are affording adversaries of all levels of sophistication the means to deliver weapon payloads and conduct ISR.[342] For example, unmanned aerial systems have played a pivotal role in recent clashes in Syria, northern Iraq, Libya, and Nagorno-Karabakh.[343] Some fly (unmanned aerial system [UAS]), some travel on or under the surface of the water (unmanned surface vessel [USV]) or unmanned underwater vessel [UUV]), and some travel on the ground (unmanned ground vehicle [UGV]). Unmanned vehicles can utilize artificial intelligence in their operation to a greater or lesser extent (discussed further in a later section). They may require human input during the execution of tasks ("human in the loop"), operate independently but under the supervision of a human who can intervene ("human on the loop"), or be fully autonomous ("human out of the loop").[344]

UASs and UUVs are more likely than other types of unmanned vehicles to deliver WMD payloads. In general, differences between UASs and UUVs, on the one hand, and cruise missiles and torpedoes, respectively, on the other, include: 1) the former can and are used for multiple purposes, including transport, ISR, and weapon delivery, while the latter are used only for weapon delivery; 2) the former are generally re-usable, while the latter are destroyed in accomplishing their mission; 3) the former are re-callable (and thus can be returned to base before delivering a weapon payload), while the latter are one-way; and 4) some types of the former can operate for hours or days at a time while the latter generally travel to their targets as quickly as possible (though perhaps with programming to avoid interception).

As discussed above, Russia currently is developing a UUV (*Poseidon*) to deliver a nuclear warhead, so the WMD application of a UUV already is being exploited. (The *Burevestnik* system, in contrast, is a cruise missile rather than a UAS, though one that may have even greater endurance on station than even the most long-endurance reconnaissance UASs.) *Poseidon* is the only publicly reported UUV intended to be used for WMD delivery.

No UASs are known to have been used or to be in development for the purpose of delivering a WMD payload, though they could be utilized for such ends.[345] For example, the U.S. Air Force reportedly has been interested in an unmanned option for its B-21 strategic bomber, though it may not have been specifically intended for the nuclear missions of this dual-capable future delivery vehicle.[346] UASs could be outfitted with agricultural-type sprayers to disseminate chemical or biological agents over a wide area. UASs also could be flown directly into certain industrial targets, with or without explosive payloads, that could result in WMD-like effects, e.g., causing a release of dangerous chemicals from a chemical plant or storage site.[347] UASs typically deliver a smaller payload than do cruise missiles, though larger UASs are being developed and fielded that could carry larger payloads. UASs also tend to fly slower and at lower altitudes than the missiles targeted by current sophisticated air and missile defense systems, like PATRIOT.[348] To address the growing challenge of adversary UASs, the U.S. Department of Defense plans to invest at least $404 million on counter-UAS research and development and at least $83 million on procurement for fiscal year 2021.[349]

As the technology improves to coordinate and integrate attacks involving multiple unmanned systems, i.e., *en masse* (an existing capability where the drones are part of a mass flight but do not coordinate their actions with each other) and swarm (an emerging capability that uses artificial intelligence to enable drones to coordinate their actions),[350] over extended ranges, the combined effect of many systems delivering small payloads will grow, especially against soft targets. In September 2019, Iran demonstrated how a coordinated *en masse* attack of UASs and cruise missiles could temporarily knock offline a large percentage of Saudi Arabia's oil processing infrastructure despite the proximity of PATRIOT air defense systems. An *en masse* or swarm attack of UASs with chemical and biological payloads could have a potent impact. The United States, China, and Russia each is pursuing swarm technologies.[351]

A case has been made that a certain type of massed drone attack—armed, fully autonomous drone swarm (AFADS)—could itself be considered a form of WMD.[352] Zachary Kallenborn, using a definition of WMD predicated on the ability to cause mass destruction in an indiscriminate manner, offers that a large number of armed drones could be programmed to fly to and attack personnel targets with no human intervention once launched. Because the swarm acts as a single system, conceivably can be scaled to achieve any chosen threshold of mass destruction, and it is not considered possible in the foreseeable future for drones to be programmed to discriminate reliably between combatants and noncombatants, AFADS can be unleashed to kill large numbers of humans without regard to their combatant status.[353]

International discussions on the definition and control of lethal autonomous weapons systems have been taking place under the auspices of the United Nations Convention on Certain Conventional Weapons. Approximately 25 countries and 100 nongovernmental organizations have called for lethal autonomous weapons systems to be banned, but there is yet no international agreement to do so. The United States, which is not known to be developing such systems, and Russia have opposed a preemptive ban, while China has supported a ban on use (but not development).[354] Former U.S. Secretary of Defense Mark Esper has stated that Chinese manufacturers are selling autonomous drones that they claim can conduct lethal, targeted strikes.[355] Other implications of autonomous unmanned vehicles will be discussed in a subsequent section on artificial intelligence.

Unlike the hypersonic and nuclear-propelled delivery vehicles discussed earlier, unmanned systems, in general, are available to and being used by many state and non-state actors, though larger UASs, those carrying sophisticated payloads, and those with the ability to coordinate their actions as part of swarms are more the preserve of advanced states. There is a large and growing commercial market for small UASs accessible to all actors, dominated by Chinese suppliers.[356] A 2017 analysis by the Institute for Defense Analyses of technological developments among small UASs projected that the drones would decrease in size while maintaining or even increase capabilities such as flight time, payload, range, endurance, and speed. New capabilities, like artificial intelligence, robotic technologies, sensor technologies, and enhanced audio and video, also are expected to be become available and be incorporated.[357] With the growth in commercial small UAS capabilities, the use of these systems by malign as well as benign actors can only be expected to increase, potentially with WMD effect.[358]

REMOTE SENSING

An important, ongoing development for the effectiveness of missiles and unmanned aerial vehicles, among other systems, is the expansion and improvement of remote sensing capabilities. Common to projections of the future military operating environment is the expectation that advances in sensing technology will continue to increase the detection and assessment capabilities of platforms, systems, and individuals.[359]

As Kier Lieber and Darryl Press explain, whereas "early Cold War strategic reconnaissance relied heavily on photoreconnaissance, underwater acoustics, and the collection of adversary communications ... modern sensors [also] gather data from across the electromagnetic spectrum; they employ seismic and acoustic sensors in tandem; and they emit radar at various frequencies to maximize resolution or to penetrate foliage."[360] Austin Long and Brendan Rittenhouse Green find that stealthy high altitude unmanned aerial vehicles, increased signals intelligence geolocation capability, and networked ground sensors have improved the United States' intelligence capability to track and target mobile missiles since the 1991 Gulf War.[361] Dean Wilkening observes that "hypersonic weapons guided by off-board sensors or advanced seekers" may leave mobile missiles vulnerable despite concerted efforts to hide them.[362]

Systems that rely on mobility, concealment, and deception for their survivability, such as mobile missiles and submarines, may be more vulnerable to detection, tracking, and interdiction than is commonly understood, and their vulnerability may increase with further advances and wider deployment of sensors and associated interpretive capabilities. This is not about a singular breakthrough technology, like one that would make the oceans transparent, although future developments in such areas as quantum systems could be transformative. Rather, it involves advances in numerous technologies, the increasing availability of data from many types of sensors, and focused collection and analysis efforts over time.[363] Ensuring that second-strike capabilities remain secure will require continuing cognizance of and adaptation to new technological developments and operational constructs bearing on survivability.[364]

These remote sensing capabilities are also critically important to conventional operations and are expected to enable states that possess them increasingly to be able to hold a wider range of non-nuclear targets at risk, reducing the protection afforded by mobility, camouflage, concealment, and deception.

SOME ADDITIONAL IMPLICATIONS FOR STRATEGIC STABILITY

The expanding speed, range, and precision of conventional strike systems, especially missiles, but also counter-space and cyber weapons, means that more can be accomplished with them without resort to nuclear weapons, but this could entail significant challenges for escalation and strategic stability. Two more such challenges will be discussed here: entanglement and geostrategic context.

Entanglement

The greater speed of hypersonic missiles will afford less time to national command authorities to gather and process information and make response decisions to detected launches.[365] That challenge will be aggravated by uncertainty arising from entanglement, which refers to ambiguity as to whether an adversary's military system is conventional or nuclear. Entanglement arises when the same delivery platform can carry both conventional and nuclear payloads (i.e., dual-use platforms), but the payload of specific systems is not known. It also may occur when the same command and control (e.g., operational headquarters) or early warning systems (e.g., satellites, radars) control or provide warning for both conventional and nuclear systems. Even if systems are unambiguously conventional or nuclear, entanglement may arise if they are co-located. In cases of entanglement, an actor may target a conventional system, but its adversary may experience or at least perceive an attack on its nuclear capability, which could provoke more escalatory responses, such as launch on warning of nuclear strike systems.[366] A state might even seek to exploit entanglement as a way to deter an adversary, which could backfire if the state and its adversary do not perceive the situation in the same way.[367]

Entanglement is not a new phenomenon but is exacerbated by new developments. The United States, Russia, and China already field aircraft that can deliver nuclear or conventional payloads, and China is developing its first long-range strategic bomber. Russia also possesses nuclear torpedoes and depth charges that could be deployed on naval vessels that primarily feature conventional weapons systems. The United States has not yet clarified on what types of naval vessels it plans to deploy the nuclear armed, sea-launched cruise missile (SLCM) it currently is pursuing. While these powers' ICBMs hitherto have been exclusively nuclear armed, Russia and China also field ground-launched missiles of lesser range that are both nuclear and conventionally armed. With the INF Treaty's end, Russia is likely to deploy dual-use ground-launched, INF-range missiles, as the 9M729 already may be. The utility of hypersonic missiles for all sorts of rapid strikes as well as for penetrating missile defenses can be expected to lead Russia and China to develop conventional as well as nuclear variants of such systems.[368] Russia and China also may not trust that the United States is only interested in conventional hypersonic missiles, particularly if such systems are not part of an agreed verification regime.

Space may be the area where entanglement and its risks will be most significant. Satellites are only becoming more important to the conduct of all forms of military operations as well as to a myriad of civilian functions. It is widely assumed that the next major conflict between advanced countries will include, and may well start with, attacks on or other interference with satellites. Denying or reducing the United States' ability to leverage space assets is considered part of China's and Russia's A2/AD strategies. Attacks against satellites intended to detect and provide early warning of ballistic missile launches would be most concerning and escalatory as the United States, Russia, and/or China could interpret such attacks as a prelude to large-scale nuclear attack. But destruction of, or interference with, other satellites that relay communications; provide position, navigation, and timing functions; or enable other forms of situational awareness also could impact both nuclear and conventional operations and be viewed as critical by affected powers. As the strategic threat posed by long-range cruise missiles and glide vehicles grows relative to that posed by strategic ballistic missiles, these other satellites will be more important to their detection, tracking, and response.[369]

Geostrategic Context

The end of the INF Treaty frees the United States and Russia to join other powers in developing and deploying ground-launched, INF-range ballistic and cruise missiles. Hypersonic systems pair speed and maneuverability to an unprecedented extent. Nuclear-propelled systems, if realized, would afford virtually unlimited endurance and direction of attack. Unmanned systems provide additional platforms for ISR and weapons delivery. Combined with advances in precision guidance and remote sensing, states possessing such capabilities could hold more of an adversary's military and critical infrastructure assets at risk without resort to nuclear strikes. This may make such powers more willing to test the nuclear thresholds of nuclear-armed adversaries, with attendant risks of miscalculation and escalation. This could be particularly pertinent to the unique circumstances of the contemporary U.S.-China military rivalry in the Indo-Pacific theater as compared to those that pertained to the U.S.-Soviet stand-off in Europe during the Cold War and its echoes in the current U.S.-Russian competition.

In Europe during the Cold War, the United States faced a conventional and nuclear military peer adversary in the Soviet Union on a continent where the Soviet Union was perceived as poised to march into and seize control of the world's most significant concentration of advanced industrial resources. The United States viewed preventing this to be a vital interest, as it did not believe that it could long maintain its own way of life if a hostile power controlled the resources and geography of the Eurasian landmass. The same calculation led the United States to intervene in the two world wars of the twentieth century. After those wars, this was a conviction accepted broadly by the U.S. body politic—or at least those who closely followed and most influenced U.S. national security and foreign policy—and provided the foundation upon which the United States formally committed itself to Europe's defense through NATO, even at the risk of nuclear war. It also was a commitment credible to the Soviet Union, which itself viewed the rivalry as existential. Russia is less able and presumably inclined to pose the same threat to the United States in Europe that the Soviet Union did, but support for NATO remains ingrained among the U.S. public.[370]

In contrast, China is not poised to seize control of the Eurasian landmass. Seas also separate it from Japan and Australia, two of the United States' three major allies in the Indo-Pacific theater (i.e., those who enjoy the protection of the U.S. nuclear umbrella), though not the third, South Korea. The territories at most risk of Chinese aggression and conquest for at least the next decade are islets, shoals, and disputed waters in the South China Sea, the disputed Senkaku Islands (Diaoyu to China) in the East China Sea that are administered by Japan, and Taiwan.

The stakes for the United States here are far less than in Europe during the Cold War. The United States has extended no formal security guarantees to most of the parties disputing territory in the South China Sea with China, and, while it has a mutual defense treaty with the Philippines, that country (like Thailand, another regional U.S. treaty ally) is not recognized as being under the U.S. nuclear umbrella. The United States also does not maintain formal diplomatic relations or have a mutual defense agreement with Taiwan, and the 1979 Taiwan Relations Act only obligates the United States to make available to Taiwan the means of self-defense. Only the dispute over the uninhabited Senkaku islands involves territory falling within the scope of a formal security agreement with an ally (Japan) who is covered by the U.S. nuclear umbrella. Even in this case, though, the United States has not taken a position on the sovereignty dispute and presumably would be less inclined to escalate to the nuclear level a military conflict with China involving only those uninhabited islets, as opposed to Chinese aggression more directly threatening the sovereignty and survival of its major regional allies (Japan, South Korea, and Australia).

There is no question that the United States perceives important interests at stake in the South China Sea, East China Sea, and Taiwan. The United States is particularly concerned that if it cannot keep China from consolidating its claims in these areas, it will cede to China its dominant position in the larger region, lose allies and influence, and embolden China to press other interests. The United States has conveyed through words and deeds a preparedness to use force to protect its interests in the region. For example, the United States recently explicitly rejected China's claim to sovereignty over the South China Sea, reaffirmed that its mutual defense agreement with Japan covers the Senkaku Islands, sent the first Cabinet-level official to Taiwan to meet with its president, and increased freedom-of-navigation patrols in disputed waters and airspace. But the threats that China poses in the South China Sea, East China Sea, and Taiwan are of less direct and obvious relevance to the United States' vital interest in preventing one power from dominating the resources and geography of the Eurasian landmass than a Soviet invasion of Western Europe would have been. Moreover, military conflict with China in those areas would play out over vast expanses of water and the air and orbital space above them, with less prospect of collateral damage to civilian populations than would any war occurring in Europe (or in South Korea, Japan's main islands, or Australia).

While the United States enjoys clear military superiority, China is not able to pursue its claims in these areas by the credible threat or actual use of military force. But the military situation is becoming more contestable as China modernizes its forces. China's development of a larger and more survivable nuclear force should increase its confidence that the United States could not negate its ability to inflict unacceptable destruction upon the U.S. homeland, while new conventional capabilities, including hypersonic missiles but also cyber and space assets, provide it with more means to counter U.S. opposition without resort to nuclear weapons. The United States also will be able to employ advanced conventional capabilities as it moves to deter and defeat Chinese aggression, and it will be aware that China, with its much smaller nuclear force geared toward countervalue deterrence, will have fewer nuclear escalation options under the current composition of its forces.

Both might find reason to believe that they could achieve limited aims in a conflict waged largely in the sea, air, and space domains with advanced conventional systems and without provoking nuclear war. While the risk of nuclear escalation cannot be eliminated and must be keenly felt, the collateral damage of a conventional conflict should be less extensive and the stakes will be less vital, especially for the United States, than a major conflict in Europe. If China were prevailing in a conventional fight over Taiwan or disputed territories in the South or East China Seas, the United States would have to weigh the risks of initiating nuclear strikes against falling back to the defense of its more vital regional interests, the security of its major treaty allies. If the United States were prevailing, China would have the option to stand down to fight another day and to justify its action as a strategic retreat in a longer struggle with the U.S. "hegemon," though there are questions as to whether its regime could endure the humiliation of defeat. There is some indication that Chinese strategists discount the possibility of conventional war with the United States escalating to the nuclear level.[371] If China's leadership holds such views, it could misinterpret U.S. signals intended to convey resolve and precipitate escalation. It is a dangerous thing to be complacent about the risks of conflict escalating to the nuclear level.

In sum, there may be greater scope going forward for tensions between China and the United States in the Indo-Pacific region leading to direct conflict than there was for U.S-Soviet tensions in Europe during the Cold War, and still today with Russia, because it is more conceivable that the conflict can remain conventional. As both combatants possess nuclear weapons, the risk of nuclear escalation cannot be eliminated, though. Factors such as entanglement and national leaders on both sides being less steeped on nuclear risks than U.S. and Soviet leaders were during the Cold War are likely to aggravate that risk. If nuclear use does occur, it is more likely to be limited if it occurs at sea or in space, but it should be expected to escalate if impacting the homelands or strategic deterrent forces of the combatants, as well as the territory and population centers of U.S. major treaty allies in the region.

It is sobering to contemplate that the Indo-Pacific theater could be the site of the first major war between great powers in the nuclear age. It should concentrate minds on both sides about the risks of pursuing interests, taking actions, and employing rhetoric that aggravate tensions, and motivate them to engage in direct discussions to clarify and mitigate those risks.

OTHER EMERGING OR DISRUPTIVE TECHNOLOGIES

This paper lastly will look at four other emerging or disruptive technologies that may significantly impact the future nature and role of WMD but were not addressed in the 2014 paper (artificial intelligence [AI] and quantum systems) or were given only a glance (biotechnology and additive manufacturing [AM]).[372] They are not WMD technologies *per se* but broad enabling ones with many civilian and military applications, only some of which concern WMD. Their influence already is being felt, though their direct impact on WMD may not manifest until beyond this paper's 2030 horizon. AI, biotechnology, and quantum systems also are explicit areas of great power competition.

While AI, biotechnology, quantum systems, and AM are discussed individually below, each also will converge with aspects of the others. For example, AI will be important to gleaning insights from relevant data sets to advance biotechnology, quantum systems, and AM. These four technologies also will converge with other emerging or disruptive technologies that are not addressed here, including cyber, 5G, space, and nano.[373] More thorough treatments of how emerging and converging technologies may impact WMD are available elsewhere.[374]

ARTIFICIAL INTELLIGENCE

"AI refers to the ability of machines to perform tasks that normally require human intelligence – for example, recognizing patterns, learning from experience, drawing conclusions, making predictions, or taking action – whether digitally or as the smart software behind autonomous physical systems."[375] AI is sometimes disaggregated into "general AI" and "narrow AI." General AI would match or outperform the ability of a human to understand its environment and act on its own based on that understanding. It is the type of AI that generates fear of machines "taking over" and is depicted in movies like *2001: A Space Odyssey* and the *Terminator* series. There is debate as to whether General AI will ever be attainable and consensus that if it is, it would be well into the future.[376] Narrow AI, one form of which is referred to as machine learning, executes complex tasks but is "brittle in nature" in that it is limited by its programming and works reliably only for the "intended tasks and operating environment." [377] It has been around for years and is becoming increasingly capable, including by having much more data to be trained on as a result of digitalization.[378] Narrow AI is central to such things as smart speakers (e.g., *Alexa*), facial recognition software, and self-driving vehicles, along with their military and security analogues. Narrow AI is what is relevant to the time horizon of this paper.

The United States, China, and Russia each has accorded high priority to the further development of AI. In 2020, U.S. Secretary of Defense Mark Esper said, "unlike advanced munitions or next-generation platforms, artificial intelligence is in a league of its own, with the potential to transform nearly every aspect of the battlefield."[379] In 2018, the U.S. Defense Department established a Joint Artificial Intelligence Center (JAIC) to accelerate the development and adoption of AI,[380] and the following year, President Trump signed an executive order for an *American Artificial Intelligence Initiative*.[381] In 2017, China announced its *New Generation Artificial Intelligence Development Plan* with a goal of becoming the world leader in AI by 2030.[382] That same year, Russian President Putin grandly stated, "Whoever becomes the leader in this sphere will become ruler of the world."[383] In late 2019, Russia unveiled its own *National Strategy for the Development of Artificial Intelligence through 2030*.[384]

AI will be applied to ever-expanding streams of data from all types of systems and for all kinds of purposes. It is hard to imagine a capability to which AI is not or could not be applied. For example, the use of AI algorithms to sift and analyze increasing streams of data generated by growing numbers and types of sensors promises to improve target detection and geolocation for missiles and other munitions as well as guidance to the targets.[385] AI also will be central to the further development of autonomous systems, including enabling swarm attacks wherein individual unmanned systems will be able to communicate with each other and to adjust and optimize their role in the attack based on conditions encountered in real time.[386] AI additionally should facilitate detection, tracking, discrimination, and interception of incoming missiles by missile defense systems.[387]

AI may confer decisive advantages to technological leaders. Referring to AI-enabled autonomous systems, former Deputy Secretary of Defense Robert Work finds that it will likely "increase the quality and speed of decisions in time-critical operations … enable new missions that would otherwise be impossible … [and] help restore conventional overmatch and thereby strengthen conventional deterrence."[388] AI is an integral part of the Third Offset Strategy that Dr. Work championed while deputy secretary to extend U.S. military superiority, and as the current leader in AI, the United States is well positioned to exploit it to that end. However, AI also has raised concerns for strategic stability, posing risks to both AI leaders and laggards. Among those concerns are the perceived security of strategic deterrent forces, the speed of decision-making, and greater reliance on unmanned systems making war more likely.

New and enhanced capabilities enabled by AI will emerge gradually and cut both ways, impacting offensive and defensive postures and one's own and adversaries' systems. There will be the tendency, as always, to assume the worst about adversaries' capabilities while accentuating one's own weaknesses. Most significantly, these tendencies will heighten concerns about an AI-enabled state's ability to compromise its adversary's strategic deterrent. As Zachary Davis observes,

> AI-empowered ISR that makes it possible to locate, track, and target a variety of enemy weapons systems raises the possibility of striking strategic assets… This capability, and perceptions of its existence, could disrupt long-held assumptions about deterrence stability, especially if it appeared possible to conduct a disarming counterforce strike against an adversary's retaliatory forces…. Even the perception of an imbalance that favors striking first can lead to misperception, miscalculation, and arms racing.[389]

Edward Geist and Andrew J. Lohn find "Russia and China already may believe that the United States is attempting to leverage AI to threaten the survivability of their strategic nuclear forces."[390] So, although it would be a tremendous leap of confidence for a nuclear weapons state with AI-enhanced counterforce capabilities to risk initiating nuclear war through a preemptive attack against its nuclear-armed rival, the fear that one's adversary may have such confidence will drive compensating actions. Some of those compensating actions may be destabilizing, like launch-on-warning postures in a technological environment where warning time and reliability are reduced.

AI will be increasingly necessary to sift through and make sense of ever-growing streams of data from a myriad of sensors. Decision makers will tend to become more reliant on AI insights when making decisions and may even feel the need to delegate some strategically significant response to AI-enabled systems—for instance, when facing attack by fast-moving hypersonic missiles. But AI is only as good as the data sets it is trained on. Data sets may be insufficient to enable reliable analysis; they may be compiled in ways that reflect humans' unconscious biases,[391] resulting in suboptimal analyses; and/or the data may be corrupted deliberately or inadvertently. As previously mentioned, narrow AI is brittle in nature and can be rendered ineffective by even small anomalies in information, whether naturally occurring or intentionally introduced (hacking or spoofing), that a human brain could recognize and discount.[392] Trust in the data will be a key decision factor in determining whether and how to utilize AI. Trust in how the AI analyzes the data also will be important given that AI will be a "black box" to most users.[393] Much will be at stake. As the Defense Innovation Board observed, "Time pressures on the development and deployment of poorly understood systems could lead to unintended outcomes, such as emergent effects of tightly coupled systems, accidents, or unintended engagements leading to international instability (e.g., a "flash war").[394]

Such concerns have focused attention on ethical questions arising from AI. Several sets of principles were promulgated in recent years to guide AI development and utilization, including by the Future of Life Institute (2017), the European Commission's High-Level Expert Group on Artificial Intelligence (2019), the Organization for Economic Co-operation and Development (2019), and the Beijing Academy of Artificial Intelligence (2019). Each has emphasized "the importance of the human element to ensure legal compliance and ethical acceptability."[395] In 2020, the U.S. Department of Defense adopted five ethical principles for its emergent use of AI: AI systems must be 1) responsible (utilizing appropriate levels of judgment and care); 2) equitable (to minimize unintended bias); 3) traceable (understanding how the "black box" works); 4) reliable (explicit, well-defined uses subjected to testing and assurance); and 5) governable (designed to fulfill intended functions while possessing the ability to detect and avoid unintended consequences).[396] Applying ethical principles in specific cases of AI development and application will be an inherently subjective and contentious endeavor.

The increasing use of unmanned systems, especially UASs, is putting fewer human operators at risk of physical injury or death. AI is expected to enable a significant expansion in the use of unmanned vehicles of all types and for many purposes.[397] Recent experience and common sense suggest that states are more tolerant of the loss of unmanned than manned aircraft. For example, in terms of recent experience, the United States chose not to conduct a retaliatory airstrike after Iran shot down a U.S. Global Hawk surveillance drone in June 2019, with the U.S. leadership indicating that it believed the cost in Iranian lives lost would have been a disproportionate response.[398]

Concern has been expressed, though, that the reduction in the risk to human combatants arising from continuing substitution of unmanned vehicles for manned ones may make it easier for states to resort to the use of force. In 2019, an expert from China's People's Liberation Army (PLA) stated that AI-enabled unmanned systems will make conventional conflict between great powers more likely by reducing the political costs of war (because of fewer casualties). He also indicated they would reduce the likelihood of conventional conflict escalating to nuclear war.[399] Erik Gartzke holds that the "[l]ower (human) cost of [technological] war leads to increased aggression" against noncombatants as "costless war does not serve the purposes of war."[400] If Gartze is correct, then the overall human costs of war will not be reduced by unmanned systems, but just skewed toward civilians. But if the PLA expert reflects Chinese leaders' views, the risk of conventional conflict between countries such as the United States and China is likely to increase, consistent with the observation made at the end of the previous section of this paper.

AI may pose other security dilemmas as well as opportunities. Deterrence fundamentally is about influencing a (human) adversary's thinking. That is hard enough to do. But what if more strategically-significant decision-making, such as when and where to strike, is delegated to AI systems? How do you understand and influence an AI system's actions? AI also may be used to generate deceptive images, e.g., a "deep fake" video of an adversary leader's communication, that could create false perceptions of an adversary's intent and actions. The Defense Innovation Board notes, "States frequently are able to communicate their intentions through various forms of signaling, such as explicit threats, arms build-ups, or actual military exercises. For DoD AI applications, many of these assumptions may not hold true. Signaling may be more difficult or misperceived at greater rates, knowledge of capabilities or intent is harder to discern, and the source of AI attacks at a distance and in digital forms may be harder to attribute."[401]

Other aspects of AI that some experts believe could enhance nuclear stability include faster and more reliable early warning and ISR tools; increased protection and maintenance of nuclear weapons; faster development of more survivable delivery systems; more advanced simulation and wargaming activities; and new means for monitoring and verification of arms control and disarmament.[402] The OPCW's Scientific Advisory Board has highlighted the potential applications of AI for, *inter alia*, "exploring scientific literature, predicting chemical properties, … chemical discovery, and designing chemical synthesis routes."[403] AI also could support countering WMD efforts in such ways as combining open-source trade and financial data with various intelligence sources to gain insight about illicit technology transfers, proliferation networks, and associated evasion efforts.[404]

BIOTECHNOLOGY

Many experts believe that the accelerating pace of progress in the biological sciences and greater awareness of the contributions made by biotechnology to the economy are changing the threat landscape in two ways: 1) new scientific developments are further reducing the technical barriers to the production and dissemination of biological weapons, including enabling the creation of new and even more dangerous biological agents; and 2) knowledge of biological systems particularly is growing, reflected not only in ever larger datasets of genomic information but in our ability to link that data to the biological processes associated with the pathogen-host interaction. In addition, the combination of increasingly powerful computational tools and robotic systems enable accelerated research in ways inconceivable only a few years ago.[405] Such developments, which have played a critical role in addressing the COVID-19 pandemic, also open pathways for more effective misuse of biology in new and innovative ways. This could involve modification of known pathogens, such as by enhancing virulence and environmental stability, or by enabling an agent to evade the effects of vaccines or other medical countermeasures. Perhaps more disturbing is the prospect that a novel biological agent might be able to selectively target subpopulations or even specific individuals.[406]

Recent discussions have focused on the impact of synthetic biology in general and CRISPR gene editing particularly. In its essence, "synthetic biology aims to improve the process of genetic engineering…where the design of genetic systems and the idiosyncrasies of DNA are decoupled, and one can compose living systems by mixing-and-matching genetic parts."[407] Synthetic biology is a subset of biotechnology focused specifically on the modification of microorganisms or even the creation of totally new ones and focuses on efforts to make genetic engineering more predictable by using standardized components, computer design, and conceptual approaches.[408] CRISPR is a gene editing technology, adapted from the system used by bacteria to defend against viral infections, that allows easier and more precise modification of genetic material than was possible using earlier techniques. The rapid development and exploitation of CRISPR in its various forms surprised the national security community, raising concerns that it enabled the creation of new biological warfare capabilities by both state and non-state actors.[409] Yet, exploitation of biotechnology, and synthetic biology in particular, has generated enormous societal benefits, accounting for around five percent of the U.S. economy in 2016, including in the fields of agriculture, biomedicine, and industry, and this impact is expected to grow.[410]

It is not yet clear which developments in synthetic biology will pose the greatest potential dangers. In some cases, exploitation of advances in biotechnology raise ethical or environmental concerns but do not necessarily impact national security. In other instances, there may be national security implications not related to concerns about WMD. Thus, ethicists and biologists worry about the implications of genetically modifying human DNA to correct genetic defects or impact desired new characteristics, but even when such concerns have a national security implication (such as the possible creation of "super soldiers"), they do not appear related to WMD. Similarly, the development of so-called "gene drives" to control dangerous insects create risks that fall outside the scope of this study. (Gene drives involve the editing of genetic material to ensure that the modifications are transmitted to offspring and that insects with the new characteristics come to predominate.) Again, while there may be national security impacts from use of such a technique, it is unclear that they raise significant WMD issues.[411]

The most systematic review of the national security implications of synthetic biology appeared in a 2018 report issued by a committee of the National Academies of Sciences, Engineering, and Medicine. Many potentially worrisome developments will take time to mature, while others may not fundamentally change the threat landscape. In the view of the National Academies committee, the most worrying advances relate to the ability of scientists to construct known pathogenic viruses from their genetic sequence, to produce dangerous biochemicals, and to modify known bacteria. In contrast, the committee was less concerned about the near-term potential for the artificial production of existing bacteria or the generation of totally new disease-causing organisms.[412]

One particular concern is the possible creation of biological agents that could selectively target specific sub-populations based on genetic characteristics. The collection of massive data sets of genetic information is allowing scientists to ascertain the genetic differences between different groups of people. While it is probably impossible to do so with high precision, given variations in genetics and the effects of intermarriage between groups, it may be possible to develop biological agents that would preferentially affect specific subpopulations. Moreover, it may even be possible to target specific individuals, what the National Academies committee called "personalized terrorism" (in an allusion to the promise of personalized medicine).[413]

While some of these developments may benefit state biological weapons programs, it is less clear that they will enable bioterrorism. First, exploiting synthetic biology requires the involvement of people from numerous disciplines, including expertise in bioinformatics, chemistry, biophysics, and engineering.[414] Second, despite the availability of increasingly powerful tools for genetic manipulation, tacit knowledge, the understanding of processes acquired primarily through hands-on experience, remains essential.[415] Terrorist organizations rarely have the resources and organizational ability to undertake such complex, time-consuming projects.[416]

The ineffective U.S. response to a natural outbreak, the COVID-19 pandemic, raises serious questions regarding the ability of the United States to address intentional use of biological agents. Some aspects of the failure were predictable. In 2016, the Obama Administration's President's Council of Advisors on Science and Technology assessed that the United States was poorly prepared to address intentional or natural biological threats and called for substantial changes in organization, procedure, and technical strategies.[417] Unfortunately, it is evident that those deficiencies were not rectified when, just over three years later, SARS-CoV-2 (the virus that causes COVID-19) emerged as a pandemic threat. While advances in biotechnology have facilitated responses, they have been insufficient to mitigate most of the worst impacts of disease.

QUANTUM SYSTEMS

Quantum mechanics is the subfield of physics that describes the behavior of very small particles. Quantum systems exploit the unique properties of such particles, namely superposition and entanglement. Superposition, in the context of computing, refers to the characteristic of quantum bits (qubits) to be in a mixture of the 0 and 1 states at the same time, with arbitrary weightings, as long as the system is not being observed or measured. In contrast, traditional computer bits are either 0 or 1, but never both. Entanglement refers to qubits being correlated. Individually, each qubit is random, but when measured with another qubit with which it is entangled, they have definite correlations, such as always being the same state (either 00 to 11, but never 01 or 10).[418] When the quantum system is measured, the qubits are resolved into either 0s or 1s with probabilities that depend on their final weightings.[419] Superposition affords quantum computers the ability to solve certain types of problems far more rapidly than traditional computers. In addition to its role in quantum computation, entanglement affords quantum sensors exceptional high resolution, even at great distances, and quantum communications that are provably secure.

Quantum sensors have been shown to perform better than current sensors for a number of important defense applications, including using gravimeters to detect the location of special nuclear material and underground structures; maintaining timing and position accuracy when Global Positioning Systems signals may not be available or are degraded; position updates via gravity mapping for long-term submarine navigation; and enabling magnetometry to help detect underwater threats to vessels.[420] Gravimeters exploiting quantum sensing eventually may enable detection of objects and platforms that currently are hard to detect, which could make submarines more vulnerable with significant implications for strategic stability.[421] Some quantum sensors are expected to be available for DoD use this decade, but those that could have significant implications for WMD and strategic stability are likely to lie beyond 2030.[422]

Communications systems utilizing quantum keys to encrypt/decrypt data should enable far more secure data transmissions than are possible with digital keys.[423] Quantum communications cannot be hacked without leaving a telltale sign, which is not always possible to ensure through digital communications.[424] They also may be essential to the protection of data once reliable quantum computing systems are available (discussed further below).[425] Secure communications, of course, are integral to many national security missions, including command and control of nuclear weapons systems. Quantum communications suitable for DoD applications are unlikely to be available before 2030[426] but already have some civilian applications.[427] China has built a 2,000-kilometer quantum network between Beijing and Shanghai, with plans to extend it nationwide.[428] However, more technological breakthroughs, like quantum repeaters, are required before quantum communications can be widely adopted.[429]

Quantum computers could make some calculations far more quickly than is possible with classical computers and some that are beyond the capability of classical computers. One particularly impactful application would be breaking existing digital encryption methods, exposing all data protected by such methods, including highly sensitive national security secrets. However, it is very difficult to create the conditions under which quantum computers can work. U.S. firms and China have built small quantum computers that establish proof of principle but have high error rates. In 2019, the National Academies of Sciences concluded that it is impossible to project when large, error-free quantum computers will be available, or even if they can be built, but the potential significance of quantum computing is so great that China and a number of U.S. firms are making large investments in the pursuit of such a capability.[430]

ADDITIVE MANUFACTURING

Additive manufacturing (AM), sometimes referred to as 3D printing, produces items by adding layer-upon-layer of materials pursuant to a computer model.[431] This is in contrast to conventional or subtractive machining methods, which produce items by cutting away material until the final design is achieved. AM reduces the intricacies of production processes to software programs, 3D printers, and associated resins, powders, or biological materials. This affords greater flexibility, reduces waste in production, and can enable the manufacture of some items not possible using traditional subtractive or injection cast and molding means.[432] Most AM machine design and production occurs in Germany, Japan, China, and the United Kingdom; the United States is not a leading player in the field.[433]

AM has steadily advanced and in some ways could be considered more of an emerged than emerging technology. AM complements, but is unlikely to replace, traditional manufacturing methods, which tend to be more cost effective for large-scale production.[434] AM is making the rapid prototyping and fabrication of complex parts and systems accessible to a larger population,[435] including for items relevant to WMD and their delivery systems.[436] A recent UN report found the "combination of additive manufacturing and encrypted or dark web-based communications increases the risk of proliferation."[437]

When assessing the risks of WMD proliferation arising from AM technologies, however, it is necessary to consider to whom the AM technology may proliferate. The first blush concern is that AM could enable non-state actors to produce WMD on a par with state actors because requisite technical expertise will have been captured in a computer program that anyone can execute. Fortunately, it is not so simple.[438] Some essential materials currently are not available for or amenable to 3D printing. It is not possible to produce an entire nuclear, chemical, or biological weapon by plugging a computer program into a 3D printer and pressing the start button. At best, some components of weapons could be printed.[439] If the other weapons components could be acquired or produced by other means, tacit knowledge in WMD design and production still would play a role in putting all the pieces together in a useable manner.[440] Instead of enabling naive actors to produce WMD in the first place, AM is more likely to enable actors that already have technical knowledge and capabilities relevant to WMD design and production to make WMD more efficiently and in ways that would be harder for external observers to detect.[441]

Consider nuclear weapons first. There currently is no known way to print safely a fissile material core. The use of powder-bed technologies to print an enriched uranium or plutonium core would produce a criticality incident.[442] Bruce Goodwin of Lawrence Livermore National Laboratory has recommended, however, that the United States conduct further research to ascertain that other AM technologies also could not be used to print a fissile material core.[443] It should be feasible, however, to utilize AM to print centrifuges used for enriching uranium.[444]

Goodwin believes there is only an extremely small risk that non-state actors could utilize AM technology and bring other required elements together to produce a nuclear weapon. He considers it more likely that a non-nuclear weapon state would integrate AM into its efforts to develop a nuclear weapon or a hedge capability that would be harder for outsiders to detect, monitor, and assess. Existing nuclear weapons states similarly could exploit AM to reduce the profile of enhancements to their nuclear arsenals.[445] Like the United States, they also could use AM to make their nuclear weapons program, including stockpile stewardship, more efficient.[446]

In terms of chemical weapons, AM's significance generally concerns greater accessibility to the existing ability to print microreactors.[447] Microreactors synthesize chemicals at a very small-scale in a safe, efficient, and highly pure manner, and can be scaled to a limited extent. Many pharmaceutical and fine chemical compounds currently cannot be produced in microreactors, including some used in chemical weapons,[448] but other hazardous chemicals can be.[449] A variety of disposable and consumable laboratory equipment also can be printed, which can have particular utility for mobile laboratories (chemical and biological).[450] AM poses a moderate proliferation risk in some chemical weapons applications.[451]

AM may be significant for production of biological weapons going forward. By positioning certain types of cells within matrices comprising other biological substances, "bioprinters" might be utilized to create biological materials or systems, including engineered tissues or bioreactors, that could be used to test or cultivate biological agents. Production and use of such devices would be difficult to detect. However, 3D printers for biological materials currently are expensive, require high expertise, and are not as accessible as other types of 3D printers, though this may change as the technology matures.[452] Such developments would make pathogen development and production more accessible to malign actors, but other knowledge and skills would be needed to fabricate useable bioweapons.[453]

The area relevant to WMD that will be most impacted by AM in the near term is delivery systems, mainly missiles.[454] AM already is widely used in aerospace-related supply chains. Raytheon has 3D printed a missile,[455] and it has been reported that Orbital ATK has used AM to produce prototype warheads for hypersonic vehicles.[456] A U.S. aerospace contractor, Relatively Space, has printed a rocket, Terran, and is gearing up to print rocket components at scale for U.S. government customers.[457] The use of AM in the production of delivery vehicles over the next decade is likely to be the preserve of aerospace and defense firms of the leading state powers.[458]

CONCLUSION

This paper has identified significant developments since the 2014 study that bear on the nature and role of WMD in the 2030 timeframe: the shifting roles of the great powers, arms control and nonproliferation regimes under pressure, more roles for chemical and biological weapons, expanding use of financial sanctions, new types of delivery vehicles and greater scope to develop and deploy them, and other emerging and disruptive technologies. It does not purport to have addressed all relevant developments since the 2014 study; that would have required more time and a longer paper. A longer paper usefully could have delved more into developments bearing on terrorist and other state actors and those associated with missile defense, space, cyberspace, directed energy weapons, and nuclear technologies. It also could have examined more robustly the technologies addressed in this study and included a classified annex reflecting relevant intelligence and sensitive scientific and technological information, but pandemic restrictions precluded planned travel to national laboratories and limited access to classified information. These other developments commend themselves to post-pandemic research.

The developments that are addressed in this paper are significant enough. They find the United States endeavoring to adapt to a changing place in a changing world. Some of the developments are beyond the United States' direct control, including China's rise and Russia's belligerence, and some are of its own choice, including stepping back from international leadership. In all cases, though, the United States will have to choose how it approaches these developments and their implications going forward.

SIGNIFICANT DEVELOPMENTS

The emergence of more capable and assertive great power rivals combined with a United States that is more focused on its parochial interests than perhaps at any time since before World War II can be expected to lead some other states, especially some U.S. allies and partners, to explore more earnestly alternatives to reliance upon U.S. leadership and protection to ensure their security in a more uncertain world. Nuclear weapons, and perhaps other forms of WMD, are among the alternatives available to them, and there is evidence that some are considering such options.

An apparent retreat from nuclear arms control, unraveling of the JCPOA, continued expansion and enhancement of nuclear arsenals in North Korea and South Asia, and recent extensive use of chemical weapons are reducing legal, normative, and practical barriers to WMD proliferation and use. The increasing and increasingly contentious wielding of U.S. financial clout through financial sanctions is sowing the seeds of its own demise, promising to diminish over time the utility of this powerful weapon against proliferation and other bad behavior.

The end of the INF Treaty and technological and engineering advances bearing on hypersonic and unmanned systems, remote sensing, and potentially nuclear propulsion are enabling development and deployment of ways to deliver nuclear and conventional payloads over longer distances with greater speed, maneuverability, and precision. These developments are blurring the lines between nuclear and conventional operations and between strategic and operational effects. Emerging or disruptive technologies, including artificial intelligence, biotechnology, quantum systems, and additive manufacturing, are expected to enhance these capabilities, enable the creation of new ones, and make some existing capabilities more accessible.

POLICY CONSIDERATIONS

The above-delineated developments pose more challenges than opportunities for countering WMD, but the United States can make choices and pursue approaches that mitigate challenges and accentuate opportunities.

First, the United States needs to again provide leadership to states that share its values and most important interests and restore their confidence in its commitment to leadership. In a world where U.S. rivals are increasingly powerful and assertive, the United States has greater need for dependable and capable allies and partners. While international leadership comes with tangible costs and other burdens, including economic ones, there is more to gain (and hitherto has been gained) from being able to create the agenda, set the course, and marshal international political and material support for mutually beneficial outcomes.

At the same time, Washington will need to insist that allies and partners make greater contributions to collective security. It can do so by persuasively laying out the factual basis for why the United States cannot continue to bear a grossly disproportionate share of the costs and burdens (e.g., two peer competitors versus one, the more powerful one residing in the East; less tolerance for disproportionate burden sharing among the U.S. body politic) and without unfounded assertions, offensive rhetoric, punitive actions, and erratic behavior. U.S. allies and partners want this type of leadership from the United States. Most have no viable near-term alternatives to U.S. leadership and protection for their security—which explains in part why allies have been generally accommodating to heightened U.S. demands for more defense spending[459]—and are looking for evidence of that leadership from the administration resulting from the 2020 U.S. presidential elections. Providing leadership will help restore allies and partners' confidence in U.S. security guarantees and will mitigate incentives for them to pursue alternative security arrangements, which for some could include nuclear weapons or other WMD development or hedge programs.

Second, the United States will need to actively pursue dialogue and negotiations on strategic weapons systems and practices with its great power rivals and hold on to existing arrangements contributing to strategic stability until successors are in place, to the extent possible. The strategic environment is becoming more complex and unpredictable; strategic discussions and negotiations can lead to measures that increase transparency and predictability and constrain destabilizing and/or needlessly expensive developments and deployments.

The United States is right to pursue strategic discussions and negotiations with both Russia and China that cover a broader range of weapons systems and feature strong monitoring and verification provisions. China is becoming too powerful to be left out; it will weigh heavily on strategic discussions and negotiations whether it is at the table or not, so better to find a way to bring it in. This may require what Heather Williams calls "asymmetric arms control" approaches given the asymmetry between China's strategic posture and that of the United States and Russia.[460] A broader range of weapons systems, both nuclear and non-nuclear, theater and intercontinental, increasingly will bear on strategic balances and stability, so they also must be addressed in great power strategic discussions and negotiations. The United States, however, will have to be prepared to include systems that are of particular concern to its great power rivals but which the United States previously has refused to integrate into formal arms control—most notably, missile defense and conventional prompt strike systems—if it is to productively engage those countries.

All this will take time. In the meantime, the United States should agree to extend the New START treaty before it expires in February 2021 to keep in place its bilateral limits on deployed strategic nuclear systems and associated monitoring and verification measures, which contribute to predictability and stability.

Third, the United States will need to continue to oppose, and impose costs for, clear and significant violations of nonproliferation agreements and norms, like those perpetrated by Syria and Russia with their chemical weapons use, to deter further violations and shore up nonproliferation regimes. Suspected violations must continue to be investigated and attributed—and perpetrators held to account. This often is an unsatisfying endeavor given varying and always limited leverage over violators, but the effort must be made if nonproliferation regimes are to be defended. Violators must be exposed, and costs imposed, even if those penalties are unlikely to change those violators' behavior, because the audience also includes other potential violators. Positive responses need to be acknowledged (and rewarded if significant enough), and succor withheld in their absence. Thus, for example, Russia should not be invited to rejoin the G7 after being found to have employed chemical weapons for assassination on multiple occasions.

Fourth, the United States needs to reevaluate its approach to North Korea's nuclear program.[461] After decades of trying, it is increasingly apparent that the United States and like-minded nations are not able, at least at an acceptable cost, to compel or induce North Korea to eliminate a nuclear weapons program that Pyongyang considers essential to its survival. In the meantime, North Korea's nuclear weapons program grows in size, sophistication, and the ways it may be wielded. The United States may need to accord more emphasis to negotiating restrictions on the size and nature of the North Korean program than to insisting on denuclearization, as it hitherto has been defined by the United States, even if the effect is *de facto* acknowledgement of the program's enduring nature. Steps toward that end already have been taken in the summitry of the last two years and the continuing moratoria on North Korea's nuclear weapons testing and launches of long-range ballistic missiles. To suggest more flexibility on aims is not also to suggest a lessening of military and other measures to deter, defend against, and pressure North Korea, which still will be necessary to move Pyongyang toward agreeing on more achievable aims while hedging against the possibility of failure.

Fifth, the United States also needs to reevaluate its unilateral approach to preventing Iran from acquiring a nuclear weapons capability. The most significant casualty of the United States' withdrawal from the JCPOA and re-imposition, and intensification, of economic sanctions has been the loss of a rare unified and coordinated international effort to pressure Iran to rein in its nuclear program. Without it, Iran has more avenues to enable it to endure unilateral U.S. pressure while continuing its objectionable behavior. All the major powers agree Iran should not be allowed to develop nuclear weapons, and at least U.S. allies and partners also agree that Iran's other bad behavior (enabling the Assad regime, sponsoring terrorist organizations, expanding its sway in the region, etc.) must be thwarted. Those aims are more likely to be achieved through restoration of unified and coordinated action on the nuclear question. Having demonstrated it will act unilaterally to punish Iran for a range of bad behavior, the United States should now refocus on how it can come together with its erstwhile JCPOA partners on a new approach that will provide greater assurance that Iran will never acquire a nuclear weapon. This should be more than the United States simply rejoining JCPOA; Iran must also agree to more enduring and transparent limitations on its nuclear activity and a process to address other issues. As with North Korea, the United States will need to maintain military and other measures to deter, defend against, and pressure Iran to move Tehran toward agreement while guarding against the possibility of failure.

Sixth, the United States must pay more attention to the dangerous combination of expanding nuclear weapons programs and continuing, and periodically heightening, tensions in South Asia. While India-Pakistan competition and tensions—the most likely spark for a nuclear exchange in the region and perhaps anywhere in the world—currently do not involve the United States as directly as our competition and tensions with our own nuclear-armed adversaries, it is fueled in part by U.S.-Chinese rivalry, which impacts China's nuclear posture, which in turn impacts India's and Pakistan's, resulting in a reverse loop effect. An India-Pakistan conflict that escalates to the nuclear level not only would be an immense humanitarian and environmental disaster that the United States could not ignore, but it would upset the United States' growing investment in strategic alignment with India, along with Japan and Australia, to balance China's rising power.

Seventh, the United States needs to assess whether its expanding resort to financial sanctions in the pursuit of parochial and controversial aims is counterproductive. Financial sanctions are a powerful policy instrument for countering WMD proliferation as well as terrorism, human rights violations, and other national security threats. Their power derives from the dominant position of the U.S. dollar, U.S. banking institutions, and U.S. government in the international financial system. These sources of financial power also give the United States, *inter alia*, an unparalleled ability to continue to finance large fiscal deficits and the way of life enabled by such spending. If the United States is viewed by other international actors as abusing its dominant position in the international financial system, such as penalizing their citizens and firms for engaging in trade permitted under multilateral arrangements, they are more motivated to pursue workarounds to the dollarized economy, which will undermine U.S. financial power over time and the many benefits that arise from such power, including the ability to use it to counter WMD proliferation. This is already underway. In its own long-term interest, the United States should be more judicious in the use of financial sanctions, applying them for purposes shared by at least our key allies or in defense of critical national interests.

Eighth, U.S. leaders need to consider carefully what it is prepared to go to war over with great power rivals and ensure it has the U.S. public's understanding and backing for doing so. This is especially important in the Indo-Pacific theater, where the United States faces a rising peer rival with near-term designs on territory and waters that are not self-evidently vital to the United States and where geography and new types of conventional weapons may lead one or more great powers to wager that they can fight a war without escalating to the nuclear level. If the United States enjoys clear conventional military superiority and perhaps even poses a preemptive threat against China's strategic nuclear deterrent, China is not in a position to risk war by enforcing claims to sovereignty over disputed territory in the South and East China Seas and over Taiwan. But the situation is increasingly contestable, and China may grow more confident that the United States will not risk major war, and especially nuclear war, to defend interests that China may consider self-evidently more important to it than to the United States. It certainly has become more assertive in recent years in pressing its claims. If U.S. leaders consider the defense of its interests in these areas vital enough to go to war with China, perhaps because of a Munich analogy (if we do not stop China here, we will have do so later and elsewhere and at great risk and costs), they need to do more to impress that upon not just China, but the U.S. public and regional allies as well.[462] The case for war is not as self-evident as the defense of longstanding and more tangible interests in Europe, Japan, South Korea, and Australia.

Ninth, the United States must remain at the forefront of developing, utilizing, and understanding the national security implications of emerging and disruptive technologies, such as artificial intelligence, biotechnology, quantum systems, and additive manufacturing, because these technologies may dramatically impact the character of conflict, the economic fortunes of countries, and the balance of power in the international system. Emerging and disruptive technologies probably will have both stabilizing and destabilizing impacts on the development, acquisition, and use of WMD; the net impact cannot yet be discerned and will depend on decisions made along the way. They may not be mature enough to be amenable to control via international agreements, but arrangements that enhance transparency would be helpful. With regard to biotechnology, an emerging technology of particular direct relevance to one type of WMD, there is an evident requirement for the biological nonproliferation regime to have a science and technology advisory body. Comparable to the OPCW's Scientific Advisory Board, the body would closely track and advise BWC states parties on the implications of biotechnology developments for the proliferation and use of biological weapons and how they can most usefully be addressed.

Finally, this paper cannot conclude without a word on the longer-term implications of the coronavirus pandemic, which currently is impacting so many aspects of life around the globe. This pandemic has again demonstrated a harsh reality about biology that the human race has endured throughout its existence but in a way and magnitude not experienced by most people alive today. It may provide added motivation to some malign actors for the development and use of biological weapons against enemies, however they may define them. At the same time, it has shown that pandemics are indiscriminate in their effect and are as likely to disrupt or even devastate one's friends as one's adversaries. Fortunately, it also has shown how new and emerging scientific and technological capabilities can be exploited to develop medical countermeasures much faster than has been the case in the past. On balance, the net effect of the pandemic on the motivations and ability of malign actors to pursue and use biological weapons may prove to be minor, though that is not to say that the threat is insignificant. Less ambiguously, the pandemic has accentuated pre-existing deficiencies in international leadership and cooperation, but these are amenable to remedy going forward. Hopefully, the world will long remember this pandemic and prepare better for future ones, while otherwise moving on quickly once it subsides.

ABOUT THE AUTHORS

Mr. John P. Caves, Jr. is a Distinguished Fellow at the Center for the Study of Weapons of Mass Destruction, Institute for National Strategic Studies, National Defense University. He joined the Center in 2003 and served as Deputy Director from June 2013 to April 2019. Nuclear and chemical weapons threats have been the primary focus of his work. Prior to joining the Center, Mr. Caves served in the Office of the Secretary of Defense in several capacities, including as Deputy Director for Counterproliferation Policy; Country Director for Turkey, Spain, and Cyprus in the Office of European Policy; and Deputy Director for Plans in the Defense Security Assistance Agency. In 1985, he addressed nuclear weapons policy issues in the Office of the Defense Adviser, U.S. Mission to NATO. Mr. Caves twice has been awarded the Secretary of Defense Medal for Meritorious Civilian Service. His recent publications include "Fentanyl as a Chemical Weapon," in *Proceedings,* Center for the Study of Weapons of Mass Destruction (2019); "Deterrence, Escalation Management, and Countering Weapons of Mass Destruction," in *Charting a Course: Strategic Choices for a New Administration*, ed. R.D. Hooker, Jr. (2016); and *The Future of Weapons of Mass Destruction: Their Nature and Role in 2030*, co-authored with W. Seth Carus (2014). Mr. Caves has a Master of Public Affairs degree from Princeton University and a Master of Science degree from the National War College.

Dr. W. Seth Carus is Emeritus Distinguished Professor of National Security Policy at the Center for the Study of Weapons of Mass Destruction at the National Defense University. He was on NDU's faculty from 1997 through 2017, serving from 2003 to 2013 as the Center's Deputy Director. From 2001 to 2003, Dr. Carus was detailed to the Office of the Vice President at the White House, where he was the Senior Advisor to the Vice President for Biodefense. Before joining NDU, Dr. Carus worked at the Center for Naval Analyses (1994 to 1997), the Policy Planning staff in the Undersecretary of Defense for Policy, Office of the Secretary of Defense (1991 to 1994), and the Washington Institute for Near East Policy. Dr. Carus' work has focused primarily on issues related to biological and chemical warfare. His current research focuses on the history of chemical and biological warfare. He is author of *A Short History of Biological Warfare: From Pre-History to the 21ˢᵗ Century* (2017), "The History of Biological Warfare: What We Know and What We Don't" in *Health Security* (2015), and *Defining "Weapons of Mass Destruction,"* revised and updated (2012), as well as the working paper *Bioterrorism and Biocrimes: The Illicit Use of Biological Agents Since 1900* (2001). He is the co-author of *The Future of Weapons of Mass Destruction: Their Nature and Role in 2030* (2014). Dr. Carus has a PhD in International Relations from Johns Hopkins University.

ENDNOTES

1   John P. Caves Jr. and W. Seth Carus, *The Future of Weapons of Mass Destruction: Their Nature and Role in 2030*, Occasional Paper 10, Center for the Study of Weapons of Mass Destruction (Washington, DC: National Defense University Press, June 2014), https://wmdcenter.ndu.edu/Portals/97/Documents/Publications/Occasional%20 Papers/10_Future%20of%20WMD.pdf.

2   Caves and Carus, *Future of WMD*.

3   Caves and Carus, *Future of WMD*, 4-5.

4   Caves and Carus, *Future of WMD*, 4.

5   For example, see United Kingdom Ministry of Defence, *Global Strategic Trends: The Future Starts Today*, Sixth Edition (2018): 236, https://assets.publishing.service.gov.uk/government/uploads/system/uploads/attachment_data/ file/771309/Global_Strategic_Trends_-_The_Future_Starts_Today.pdf; and Jack Thompson, "China, the US, and World Order," in *Strategic Trends 2020: Key Developments in Global Affairs*, eds. Michael Haas and Oliver Thraner (Zurich, Switzerland: Center for Security Studies, 2020), 12, https://css.ethz.ch/en/publications/strategic-trends.html.

6   Jacob L. Heim and Benjamin M. Miller, "Measuring Power, Power Cycles, and the Risk of Great-Power War in the 21st Century" (Santa Monica, CA: The RAND Corporation, 2020), https://www.rand.org/pubs/research_reports/ RR2989.html.

7   Jonathan Cheng, "Gaining Ground on the U.S.," *Wall Street Journal*, 24 August 2020, https://www.wsj.com/ articles/chinas-economy-is-bouncing-backand-gaining-ground-on-the-u-s-11598280917.

8   Evan S. Medeiros, "The Changing Fundamentals of US-China Relations," *The Washington Quarterly* 42, no. 3 (Fall 2019): 103, https://www.tandfonline.com/doi/full/10.1080/0163660X.2019.1666355?scroll=top&needAccess=true

9   Daniel Tobin, "How Xi Jinping's 'New Era' Should Have Ended U.S. Debate on Beijing's Ambitions," Testimony before the U.S.-China Economic and Security Review Commission, 13 March 2020, 2-3, https://www.uscc.gov/ sites/default/files/testimonies/SFR%20for%20USCC%20TobinD%2020200313.pdf

10 See, for example, Paul Mozur, "Beijing Wants A.I. to be Made in China by 2030," *The New York Times*, 20 July 2017, https://www.nytimes.com/2017/07/20/business/china-artificial-intelligence.html; Ames Gross, "China Fast Becoming Top Player in Booming Asia Genomics Market," *MedTechIntelligence*, 22 June 2018, https://www.medtechintelligence.com/column/china-fast-becoming-top-player-in-booming-asia-genom- ics-market/; and Jeanne Whalen, "The quantum revolution is coming, and Chinese scientists are at the forefront," *The Washington Post*, 18 August 2019, https://www.washingtonpost.com/business/2019/08/18/ quantum-revolution-is-coming-chinese-scientists-are-forefront/

11 Andrew Chatzky and James McBride, "China's Massive Belt and Road Initiative," Council on Foreign Relations, updated 28 January 2020, https://www.cfr.org/backgrounder/chinas-massive-belt-and-road-initiative.

12 Chatzky and McBride, "China's Massive Belt." It is not clear how much of the estimated $200 million already spent by China was direct spending or extended as loans.

13 Tom Phillips, Oliver Holmes, and Owen Bowcott, "Beijing rejects tribunal's ruling in South China Sea case," *The Guardian*, 12 July 2016, https://www.theguardian.com/world/2016/jul/12/philippines-wins-south-china-sea-case- against-china. The 12 July 2016 decision was made by an Arbitral Tribunal constituted under Annex VII of the 1982 United Nations Convention on the Law of the Sea (*The South China Sea Arbitration Award of 12 July 2016*,

Permanent Court of Arbitration, PCA Case No 2013-19, https://docs.pca-cpa.org/2016/07/PH-CN-20160712-Award.pdf).

14 For example, in April 2020, a Chinese coast guard vessel collided with and sank a Vietnamese fishing vessel in the disputed Paracels Islands. In a separate incident, a Chinese seismic survey visit, escorted by Chinese maritime enforcement vessels, entered waters that Malaysia has designated an exclusive economic zone (Sanger, David E. Sanger, Eric Schmitt, and Edward Wong, "As Toll Preoccupies U.S., Rivals Test the Limits of American Power," *The New York Times*, 2 June 2020, p. A5, https://www.nytimes.com/2020/06/01/us/politics/coronavirus-global-competition-russia-china-iran-north-korea.html). On 13 July 2020, U.S. Secretary of State Michael Pompeo announced that the United States considered China's claims across most of the South China Sea to be unlawful (Michael R. Pompeo, "U.S. Position on Maritime Claims in the South China Sea," press statement, U.S. Department of State, https://www.state.gov/u-s-position-on-maritime-claims-in-the-south-china-sea/). In taking the position that China's claims are unlawful, Pompeo cited the 12 July 2016 decision of the Arbitral Tribunal, which found, *inter alia*, that "China's claims in the South China Sea do not include a claim to 'historic title'… over the waters of the South China Sea" (*The South China Sea Arbitration Award of 12 July 2016*, 471). Previously, the United States had emphasized that it took no position on the various sovereignty disputes in the South China Sea and urged such disputes to be resolved peacefully (Chun Han Wong, "U.S. Shifts Policy, Rejects Beijing's Maritime Claims," *Wall Street Journal*, 14 July 2020, https://www.wsj.com/articles/u-s-set-to-reject-certain-chinese-maritime-claims-in-south-china-sea-11594661229).

15 For example, see Brad Lendon and Yoko Wakatuski, "Japan says Chinese ships spend record time violating its territorial waters," *CNN*, 6 July 2020, https://www.cnn.com/2020/07/06/asia/japan-china-island-dispute-intl-hnk-scli/index.html; Michael MacArthur Bosack, "China's Senkaku Islands ambition," *Japan Times*, 12 June 2019, https://www.japantimes.co.jp/opinion/2019/06/12/commentary/japan-commentary/chinas-senkaku-islands-ambition/#.Xt6l-TpKjIU; and Tetsuo Kotani, "China steps up its offensive against the Senkaku Islands," *Japan Times*, 2 June 2020, https://www.japantimes.co.jp/opinion/2020/06/02/commentary/world-commentary/china-steps-offensive-senkaku-islands/#.Xt6lADpKjIU

16 For example, see Kathrin Hille, "Taiwan lambasts China for 'severe provocation' after air and naval drills," *Financial Times Online*, 10 September 2020, https://www.ft.com/content/9bf1c039-3222-4aa7-be37-6f01afc41ef2; Yimou Lee, "Taiwan president says Chinese drills a threat but not intimidated," Reuters, 15 April 2019, https://www.reuters.com/article/us-china-taiwan/tsai-says-chinese-drills-threaten-taiwan-but-is-not-intimidated-idUSKCN1RS03B; and Ben Blanchard and Yew Lun Tian, "U.S. Increases Support for Taiwan, China Threatens to Strike Back," *U.S. News*, 26 March 2020, https://www.usnews.com/news/world/articles/2020-03-26/us-increases-support-for-taiwan-in-recognition-battle-with-china. In July 2020, Japan issued a defense white paper expressing "grave concern" over China's incursions in the East Sea (Jon Herskovitz, "Japan Expresses 'Grave Concern' Over China's East Sea Incursions," *Bloomberg News*, 13 July 2020, https://www.bloomberg.com/news/articles/2020-07-14/japan-expresses-grave-concern-over-china-s-east-sea-incursions).

17 For a discussion of China's military modernization, see Defense Intelligence Agency, *China Military Power: Modernizing a Force to Fight and Win*, 2019, 3-6, https://www.dia.mil/Portals/27/Documents/News/Military%20Power%20Publications/China_Military_Power_FINAL_5MB_20190103.pdf. For a pictorial display of the 1 October 2019 military parade in Beijing, see "In pictures: China shows off military might at 70th anniversary parade," *BBC*, 1 October 2019, https://www.bbc.com/news/world-asia-china-49891769.

18 National Defense Strategy Commission, *Providing for the Common Defense: The Assessment and Recommendations of the National Defense Strategy Commission*, 2018, p. vi, https://www.usip.org/sites/default/files/2018-11/providing-for-the-common-defense.pdf.

19   See, for example, Raphael S. Cohen, Nathan Chandler, Shira Efron, Bryan Frederick, Eugenia Han, Kurt Klein, Forrest E. Morgan, Ashley L. Rhoades, Howard J. Shatz, and Yuliya Shokh, *Peering into the Crystal Ball: Holistically Assessing the Future of Warfare*, RB-10073-AF (Santa Monica, CA: RAND Corporation, 2020): 5, https://www.rand.org/pubs/research_briefs/RB10073.html.

20   Missy Ryan and Sudarsan Raghavan, "U.S. on sidelines in Libya fight as Russia extends reach," *The Washington Post*, 21 July 2020, p. A17, https://www.washingtonpost.com/national-security/us-remains-on-the-sidelines-in-libyas-conflict-as-russia-extends-its-reach/2020/07/17/04be5100-bf90-11ea-864a-0dd31b9d6917_story.html.

21   Regarding Russian interference in the 2016 presidential election, see Office of the Director of National Intelligence, *Assessing Russian Activities and Intentions in Recent US Elections*, Intelligence Community Assessment, ICA 2017-01D, 6 January 2017, p. ii, https://www.dni.gov/files/documents/ICA_2017_01.pdf; and Robert S. Mueller III, *Report on the Investigation into Russian Interference in the 2016 Presidential Election, Vol. 1* (Washington, DC: U.S. Department of Justice, March 2019), 1, https://www.justice.gov/storage/report.pdf. Regarding Russian, as well as Chinese and Iranian, interference in the 2020 presidential election, see William Evanina, "Statement by NSC Director William Evanina: Election Threat Update for the American Public," ODNI News Release, Office of the Director of National Intelligence, 7 August 2020, https://www.dni.gov/index.php/newsroom/press-releases/item/2139-statement-by-ncsc-director-william-evanina-election-threat-update-for-the-american-public.

22   Michael Birnbaum and Craig Timberg, "E.U.: Russians interfered in our elections, too," *The Washington Post*, 24 June 2019, https://www.washingtonpost.com/technology/2019/06/14/eu-russians-interfered-our-elections-too/.

23   Defense Intelligence Agency, *Russia Military Power*, 2017, 13, https://www.dia.mil/Portals/27/Documents/News/Military%20Power%20Publications/Russia%20Military%20Power%20Report%202017.pdf?ver=2017-06-28-144235-937

24   *Russia Military Power*, v.

25   Putin, Vladimir, Presidential Address to the Federal Assembly, Moscow, 1 March 2018, http://en.kremlin.ru/events/president/news/56957.

26   Amy F. Woolf, *Russia's Nuclear Weapons: Doctrine, Forces, and Modernization*, R45861, Congressional Research Service, 2 January 2020, pp. 1, 5-6, https://crsreports.congress.gov/product/pdf/R/R45861.

27   Ray Sanchez, "Putin boasts military might with animation of Florida nuke strike," *CNN*, 1 March 2018, https://www.cnn.com/2018/03/01/europe/putin-nuclear-missile-video-florida/index.html.

28   Nonstrategic nuclear weapons generally refer to those nuclear-capable delivery systems and weapons that are not (and have never been) covered by U.S.-Russian strategic nuclear arms control treaties.

29   A January 2020 Congressional Research Service Report observes,

> Recent analyses indicate that Russia is both modernizing existing types of short-range delivery systems that can carry nuclear warheads and introducing new versions of weapons that have not been a part of the Soviet/Russian arsenal since the latter years of the Cold War. In May, Lt. Gen. Robert P. Ashley of the Defense Intelligence Agency (DIA) raised this point in a public speech. He stated that Russia has 2,000 nonstrategic nuclear warheads and that its stockpile 'is likely to grow significantly over the next decade.' He also stated that 'Russia is adding new military capabilities to its existing stockpile of nonstrategic nuclear weapons, including those employable by ships, aircraft, and ground forces. These nuclear warheads include theater- and tactical-range systems that Russia relies on to deter and defeat NATO or China in a conflict. Russia's stockpile of non-strategic nuclear weapons [is] already large and diverse and is being modernized with an eye towards greater accuracy, longer ranges, and lower yields to suit their potential warfighting role. We assess Russia to have dozens of these systems already deployed or in development. They include, but are not limited to: short- and close-range ballistic missiles, ground-launched cruise missiles, including the 9M729 missile, which the U.S. Government determined violates

the Intermediate-Range Nuclear Forces or INF Treaty, as well as antiship and antisubmarine missiles, torpedoes, and depth charges.' It is not clear from General Ashley's comments, or from many of the other assessments of Russia's nonstrategic nuclear forces, whether Russia will deploy these new delivery systems with nuclear warheads. (Woolf, *Russia's Nuclear Weapons,* 17)

30   Woolf, *Russia's Nuclear Weapons,* 5-6. The United States currently is deploying low-yield nuclear warheads on some of its submarine-launched ballistic missiles and also pursuing a new nuclear-armed ship-launched cruise missile to disabuse any notion that Russia may have that it could use its theater-range, lower-yield nuclear weapons to conduct limited nuclear strikes in a regional war and the United States would be deterred from responding because it could not do so in kind, but only with strategic-range, higher-yield weapons (Office of the Secretary of Defense, *Nuclear Posture Review 2018*, February 2018, 17-18, https://dod.defense.gov/News/SpecialReports/2018Nuclear PostureReview.aspx).

31   Dmitry Gorenburg, "An Emerging Strategic Partnership: Trends in Russia-China Military Cooperation," *Wordpress.com*, 29 April 2020, https://russiamil.wordpress.com/2020/04/29/ an-emerging-strategic-partnership-trends-in-russia-china-military-cooperation/.

32   Gorenburg, "An Emerging Strategic Partnership."

33   The two Russian exercises were *Vostok 2018* in Russia's Far East and *Tenstr 2019* in Russia's central military district, which differ from earlier Chinese participation in military exercises with Russian troops by their size and their focus on traditional warfighting operations, vice nontraditional missions like counterterrorism, and disaster response. (Yang, Zi Yang, "Vostok 2018: Russia and China's Diverging Common Interests," *The Diplomat*, 17 September 2018, https://thediplomat.com/2018/09/vostok-2018-russia-and-chinas-diverging-common-interests/; and Holly Ellyatt, "Russia conducts massive military drills with China, sending a message to the West," *CNBC*, 17 September 2019, https://www.cnbc.com/2019/09/17/russia-conducts-tsentr-2019-military-exercises-with-china-and-india.html).

34   Andrew Osborn and Joyce Lee, "First Russian-Chinese air patrol in Asia-Pacific draws shots from South Korea," Reuters, 22 July 2019, https://www.reuters.com/article/us-southkorea-russia-aircraft/ first-russian-chinese-air-patrol-in-asia-pacific-draws-shots-from-south-korea-idUSKCN1UI072.

35   Scott Neuman, "As Relations with U.S. Sour, Xi Describes Putin as 'Best Friend' at Moscow Meeting," *NPR*, 6 June 2019, https://www.npr.org/2019/06/06/730200317/as-relations-with-u-s-sour-xi-describes-putin-as-best-friend-at-moscow-meeting.

36   For example, see Gorenburg, "An Emerging Strategic Partnership." National Intelligence Council, *Global Trends: Paradox of Progress*, NIC 2017-001, January 2017, pp. 35, 125, https://www.dni.gov/files/documents/nic/ GT-Full-Report.pdf; and *Global Strategic Trends*, 227-228.

37   Gorenburg, "An Emerging Strategic Partnership."

38   qtd. in Vladimir Isachenkov, "Putin: Russia-China military alliance can't be ruled out," Associated Press, 22 October 2020, https://apnews.com/article/ beijing-moscow-foreign-policy-russia-vladimir-putin-1d4b112d2fe8cb66192c5225f4d614c4.

39   See, for example, *Remarks by President Trump to the 74th Session of the United Nations General Assembly*, United Nations Headquarters, New York, NY, 24 September 2019, https://www.whitehouse.gov/briefings-statements/ remarks-president-trump-74th-session-united-nations-general-assembly/; and Office of the United States Trade Representative, "FACT SHEET: The President's Trade Agenda and Annual Report," 1 March 2019, https://ustr.gov/ about-us/policy-offices/press-office/fact-sheets/2019/march/fact-sheet-president%E2%80%99s-trade-agenda-and.

40   *National Security Strategy of the United States of America*, The White House, December 2017, https://www.white house.gov/wp-content/uploads/2017/12/NSS-Final-12-18-2017-0905.pdf; and *Summary of the 2018 National Defense Strategy of the United States of America*, U.S. Department of Defense, 2018, https://dod.defense.gov/ Portals/1/Documents/pubs/2018-National-Defense-Strategy-Summary.pdf.

41 Joel Trachtman, "What Aspects of the WTO is the Trump Administration Targeting for Reform?," Econofact.org, 28 January 2020, https://econofact.org/what-aspects-of-the-wto-is-the-trump-administration-targeting-for-reform

42 See Aaron Flaaen, and Justin Pierce (2019), "Disentangling the Effects of the 2018-2019 Tariffs on a Globally Connected U.S. Manufacturing Sector," Finance and Economics Discussion Series 2019-086 (Washington: Board of Governors of the Federal Reserve System): pp. 1, 6-7, https://www.federalreserve.gov/econres/feds/files/2019086pap.pdf; and Adam Taylor, "No president has used sanctions and tariffs quite like Trump," *The Washington Post*, 29 August 2018, https://www.washingtonpost.com/world/2018/08/29/no-president-has-used-sanctions-tariffs-quite-like-trump/.

43 Concerning NATO, for example, President Trump called NATO obsolete during his 2016 presidential campaign and, after becoming president, during a 15 January 2017 interview with the German newspaper *Bild*. He also declined to explicitly affirm NATO's Article 5 mutual defense guarantee during a 25 May 2017 NATO summit, when he was widely expected to have done so; instead, he criticized other allies for failing to meet their defense spending requirements. President Trump later told visiting NATO Secretary General Jens Stoltenberg on 12 April 2017 that NATO is no longer obsolete and stated his commitment to Article 5 during a visit to Poland on 9 June 2017. New controversy arose on the Article 5 issue during an 18 July 2018 interview with Fox News host Tucker Carlson when President Trump injected doubt as to his willingness to defend new NATO member Montenegro (Cyra Master, "Trump tells German paper: NATO 'obsolete'," *The Hill*, 15 January 2017, https://thehill.com/homenews/administration/314432-trump-nato-is-obsolete; Robbie Gramer, "Trump Discovers Article 5 After Disastrous NATO Visit," *ForeignPolicy.com*, 9 June 2017, https://foreignpolicy.com/2017/06/09/trump-discovers-article-5-after-disastrous-nato-visit-brussels-visit-transatlantic-relationship-europe/; Rosie Gray, "Trump Declines to Affirm NATO's Article 5," *The Atlantic*, 25 May 2017, https://www.theatlantic.com/international/archive/2017/05/Trump-declines-to-affirm-natos-article-5/528129/; Jacob Pramuk, "Trump endorses NATO's mutual defense pact in Poland, after failing to do so on first European trip," *CNBC.com*, 6 July 2017, https://www.cnbc.com/2017/07/06/trump-us-stands-firmly-behind-nato-article-5.html; "Trump says Nato 'no longer obsolete," *BBC*, 12 April 2017, https://www.bbc.com/news/world-us-canada-39585029; and Eileen Sullivan, "Trump Questions the Core of NATO: Mutual Defense, Including Montenegro," *The New York Times*, 18 July 2018, https://www.nytimes.com/2018/07/18/world/europe/trump-nato-self-defense-montenegro.html). Concerning the U.S.-ROK alliance, the Trump Administration demanded in 2019 a 50 percent increase in what the ROK contributes to the costs of stationing U.S. troops in its country, while the ROK offered only 13 percent. The impasse precluded a multi-year renewal of the governing, bilateral Special Measures Agreement (SMA), which lapsed at the end of 2019 and resulted in the furlough of more than 4,000 South Korean employees of U.S. Forces Korea (Lee Haye-ah, "U.S.-South Korea defense cost deal needs to be 'fully acceptable' to Moon, Trump—official," *Yonhap News Agency*, 14 May 2020, https://en.yna.co.kr/view/AEN20200515000251325). After a few months, the two sides agreed on another one-year extension under which the ROK agreed to contribute an additional 8 percent (Paul McLeary, "Esper Stands by Korea, Taiwan – But Offers Olive Branch to China," *BreakingDefense.com*, 21 July 2020, https://breakingdefense.com/2020/07/esper-stands-by-korea-taiwan-but-offers-olive-branch-to-china/). Concerning the U.S.-Japan alliance, there is conflicting information as to whether the United States is seeking a large increase in Japanese contributions to the costs of U.S. forces based in Japan, with former U.S. National Security Adviser John Bolton claiming that President Trump demanded Japan pay $8 billion a year, up from $2.5 billion, while Japan's Chief Cabinet Secretary Yoshihide Suga denied Bolton's claims (Seth Robson, "Japanese citizens feel anxious and concerned about U.S. alliance, security experts says," *Stars and Stripes Online*, 19 July 2020, https://www.stripes.com/news/pacific/japanese-citizens-feel-anxious-and-concerned-about-us-alliance-security-expert-says-1.638097).

44　See, for example, Anna Dimitrova, "The State of the Transatlantic Relationship in the Trump Era," Policy Paper, Fondation Robert Schuman, 4 February 2020, https://www.robert-schuman.eu/en/european-issues/0545-the-state-of-the-transatlantic-relationship-in-the-trump-era.

45　NATO has set a target of 2 percent of gross domestic product for each member to spend on defense, which Germany has failed to meet. President Trump's decision to reduce the U.S. troop presence was not communicated in advance to Berlin, other NATO allies, or the U.S. Congress (Robert Burns, "Trump announces major troop cut in 'delinquent' Germany," *Associated Press*, 15 June 2020, https://apnews.com/b4ac0b046a6be385b583a816e98f2240). Originally announced as closer to a one-quarter reduction in the U.S. force presence in Germany, a 29 July 2020 speech by Secretary of Defense Esper indicated that it would be a one-third reduction (from 36,000 to 24,000) (Mark Esper, "U.S. European Command Force Posture Policy Press Conference: Secretary Esper's Opening Statement (as prepared)," Secretary of Defense Speech, U.S. Department of Defense, 29 July 2020, https://www.defense.gov/newsroom/Speeches/Speech/Article/2292081/us-european-command-force-posture-policy-press-conference-secretary-espers-open/). Secretary Esper said the force move was to "enhance our strategic flexibility and operational unpredictability." Later that day, President Trump again cast the reduction as a response to the level of German defense spending, tweeting: "Germany pays Russia billions of dollars a year for Energy, and we are supposed to protect Germany from Russia. What's that all about? Also, Germany is very delinquent in their 2% fee to NATO. We are therefore moving some troops out of Germany!" (https://twitter.com/realdonaldtrump/status/1288620254130626561).

46　For example, Larry Hogan, Republican Governor of Maryland, recounted a private dinner that President Trump had with the Republican Governors Association in February 2020, "Then [Trump] came out and gave one of his unscripted rally speeches…I don't remember him mentioning the [corona]virus, but he talked about how much he respected President Xi Jinping of China; how much he like playing golf with his buddy 'Shinzo' [Abe, Prime Minister of Japan]; how well he got along with North Korea dictator Kim Jong Un. Then, the jarring part: Trump said he really didn't like dealing with President Moon from South Korea. The South Koreans were 'terrible people,' he said, and he didn't know why the United States had been protecting them all these years. 'They don't pay us,' Trump complained" (Larry Hogan, "Fighting alone," *The Washington Post*, p. B1, https://www.washingtonpost.com/outlook/2020/07/16/larry-hogan-trump-coronavirus/?arc404=true). Also see Chris Cillizza and Brenna Williams, "15 times Donald Trump praised authoritarian rulers," *CNN.com*, 2 July 2019, https://www.cnn.com/2019/07/02/politics/donald-trump-dictators-kim-jong-un-vladimir-putin/index.html; Tom Porter, "'Why shouldn't I like him?' Trump piled praise on Kim Jong Un in his first interview since their summit collapsed," *BusinessInsider.com*, 1 March 2019, https://www.businessinsider.com/trump-praises-kim-jong-un-vietnam-summit-2019-3; Aime Williams and Valerie Hopkins, "Trump praises Hungary's Orban in White House visit," *Financial Times*, 13 May 2019, https://www.ft.com/content/06f69c6c-75a8-11e9-bbad-7c18c0ea0201; and "Trump Praises Erdogan Despite Incidents of Violence Against Protestors," *VOA News*, 21 September 2017, https://www.voanews.com/usa/us-politics/trump-praises-erdogan-despite-incidents-violence-against-protesters.

47　Gramer, "Trump Discovers Article 5;" and "Trump says Nato 'no longer obsolete."

48　Matthew J. Burrows and Peter Engelke, *What World Post-COVID-19? Three Scenarios* (Washington, DC: Atlantic Council, April 2020), 6, https://atlanticcouncil.org/content-series/shaping-post-covid-world-together/what-world-post-covid-19-three-scenarios/.

49　Office of the Press Secretary, "FACT SHEET: U.S. Response to the Ebola Epidemic in West Africa," The White House, 16 September 2014, https://obamawhitehouse.archives.gov/the-press-office/2014/09/16/fact-sheet-us-response-Ebola-epidemic-west-africa.

50　Burrows and Engelke, 6.

51　Donald J. Trump, Letter to Dr. Tedros Adhanom Ghebreyesus, Director-General of the World Health Organization, The White House, 18 May 2018, https://www.whitehouse.gov/wp-content/uploads/2020/05/Tedros-Letter.

pdf?fbclid=IwAR37I6eg33gvIDfse0-iLERvoNLTGVpLNdt31uK_AEs5OMiFNZCJLxJkuds; and Sara Murray, Zachary Cohen, Kylie Atwood, and Vivian Salama, "Trump administration informs Congress it is withdrawing from World Health Organization," *CNN.com*, 7 July 2020, https://www.cnn.com/2020/07/07/politics/us-withdrawing-world-trade-organization/index.html. Under the terms of its membership in the WHO, the United States' withdrawal will be effective one year after its 6 July 2020 formal withdrawal notification.

52   Emily Rauhala and Yasmeen Abutaleb,'"U.S. says it won't join WHO-linked effort to develop, distribute coronavirus vaccine," *The Washington Post*, 2 September 2020, https://www.washingtonpost.com/world/coronavirus-vaccine-trump/2020/09/01/b44b42be-e965-11ea-bf44-0d31c85838a5_story.html. On 9 October 2020, China announced that it would participate (Gerry Shih and Emily Rauhala, "China joins WHO-backed vaccine plan that White House spurned," *The Washington Post*, 9 October 2020, https://www.washingtonpost.com/world/asia_pacific/coronavirus-vaccine-china-covax-who/2020/10/08/cf4e1e96-09d2-11eb-8719-0df159d14794_story.html).

53   See, for example, Katrin Bennhold, "'Sadness' and Disbelief from a World Missing American Leadership," *The New York Times*, 23 April 2020, https://www.nytimes.com/2020/04/23/world/europe/coronavirus-american-exceptionalism.html; and Kevin Rudd, "The world after covid-19, By invitation: Kevin Rudd on America, China and saving the WHO," *The Economist Online*, 15 April 2020, https://www.economist.com/by-invitation/2020/04/15/kevin-rudd-on-america-china-and-saving-the-who. A Congressional Research Service report on the potential implications of COVID-19 noted, "Some observers have focused on the possibility that the COVID-19 pandemic could cause or accelerate a decline or erosion in the U.S-led liberal international order that has operated since World War II, in the international institutions and norms that contribute to it, and consequently in global governance." See Ronald O'Rourke, Kathleen J. McInnis, and Michael Moodie, *COVID-19: Potential Implications for International Security Environment—Overview of Issues and Further Reading for Congress*, CRS Report R46336, Congressional Research Service, p. 1, https://crsreports.congress.gov/product/pdf/R/R46336.

54   Emily Rauhala and Karen DeYoung, "U.S. experts at WHO chronicled virus's rise," *The Washington Post*, 20 April 2020, p. A1, https://www.washingtonpost.com/world/national-security/americans-at-world-health-organization-transmitted-real-time-information-about-coronavirus-to-trump-administration/2020/04/19/951c77fa-818c-11ea-9040-68981f488eed_story.html.

55   *Transatlantic Trends 2020*, Bertelsmann Foundation, The German Marshall Fund of the United States, and Institut Montaigne, 2020, p. 9, https://www.gmfus.org/sites/default/files/TT20_Final.pdf.

56   *Transatlantic Trends 2020*, 18.

57   Malcolm Chalmers and Will Jesset, *Defence and the Integrated Review: A Testing Time*, RUSI Whitehall Report 2-20 (London: Royal United Services Institute for Defence and Security Studies, March 2020), p. 3, https://rusi.org/publication/whitehall-reports/defence-and-integrated-review-testing-time.

58   Another perspective on the loosening of U.S. ties to its post-World War II allies and security partners is provided in a RAND report, which observes: "U.S. adversaries—China, Russia, Iran, North Korea, and terrorist groups—likely will remain constant [between now and 2030], but U.S. allies are liable to change as Europe becomes increasingly fragmented and inward-looking and as Asia reacts to the rise of China" (*Peering into the Crystal Ball*, 16).

59   The role of the United States in dissuading nuclear and other WMD proliferation is discussed throughout the 2014 paper, particularly pages 13, 17, 33, and 38-40. Also see, for example, Pete McKenzie, "America's Allies are Becoming Nuclear Proliferation Threat," *DefenseOne.com*, 25 March 2020, https://www.defenseone.com/threats/2020/03/americas-allies-are-becoming-nuclear-proliferation-threat/164057/; and Eric Brewer, *Toward a More Proliferated World? The Geopolitical Forces that Will Shape the Spread of Nuclear Weapons*, a joint product of the Center for a New American Security and the Center for Strategic and International Studies, September 2020, pp. 16-18, https://www.csis.org/analysis/toward-more-proliferated-world.

60   Maggie Haberman and David E. Sanger, "Transcript: Donald Trump Expounds on His Foreign Policy Views," *New York Times*, 26 March 2016, https://www.nytimes.com/2016/03/27/us/politics/donald-trump-transcript.html; and Stephanie Condon, "Donald Trump: Japan, South Korea might need nuclear weapons," *CBSNews.com*, 29 March 2016, https://www.cbsnews.com/news/donald-trump-japan-south-korea-might-need-nuclear-weapons/.

61   "MBS: Saudis will pursue nuclear weapons if Iran does," *Al Jazeera*, 15 May 2018, https://www.aljazeera.com/news/2018/03/mbs-saudis-pursue-nuclear-weapons-iran-180315152433732.html.

62   In 2008, the United States and Saudi Arabia signed a memorandum of agreement to cooperate on nuclear activities for peaceful purposes. Despite years of discussions, the two countries have not been able to conclude an agreement under section 123 of the (U.S.) Atomic Energy Act that is required for the United States to engage in significant nuclear cooperation with foreign governments. The United States wants Saudi Arabia to agree to terms similar to those the United States earlier agreed with the United Arab Emirates (UAE), which exclude UAE from acquiring uranium enrichment and plutonium reprocessing capabilities. UAE also has concluded an Additional Protocol with the International Atomic Energy Agency (IAEA). (In 2020, the UAE became the first Arab country to complete a nuclear reactor to generate power.) Saudi Arabia is also cooperating with other countries in its development of a civilian nuclear program, including Argentina, Russia, China, South Korea, and France, and has solicited international bids to construct two nuclear reactors. In 2020, the *Wall Street Journal* reported that the Saudis had built with Chinese help, but not disclosed, a facility for milling of uranium oxide ore to produce "yellowcake," the precursor material for enriched uranium. Saudi Arabia denies the report. The report nonetheless has intensified interest within the U.S. Congress in restricting nuclear cooperation with Saudi Arabia (Christopher M. Blanchard and Paul K. Kerr, "Prospects for Enhanced U.S.-Saudi Nuclear Energy Cooperation," *In Focus*, IF10799, Congressional Research Service, updated 13 August 2020, https://crsreports.congress.gov/product/pdf/IF/IF10799; Warren P. Strobel, Michael R. Gordon, and Felicia Schwartz, "Saudi Arabia, with China's Help, Expands Its Nuclear Program," *The Wall Street Journal*, 4 August 2020, https://www.wsj.com/articles/saudi-arabia-with-chinas-help-expands-its-nuclear-program-11596575671; and "U.S. 'Scrutinizing' Saudi Arabia's Nuclear Program After Chinese Help," *Haaretz*, 7 August 2020, https://www.haaretz.com/us-news/saudi-arabia-reportedly-expands-nuclear-program-with-china-s-help-1.9049176).

63   "Erdogan says that it's unacceptable that Turkey can't have nuclear weapons," Reuters, 4 September 2019, https://www.reuters.com/article/us-turkey-nuclear-erdogan/erdogan-says-its-unacceptable-that-turkey-cant-have-nuclear-weapons-idUSKCN1VP2QN

64   Michelle Ye Hee Lee, "More than ever, South Koreans want their own nuclear weapons," *The Washington Post*, 13 September 2017, https://www.washingtonpost.com/news/worldviews/wp/2017/09/13/most-south-koreans-dont-think-the-north-will-start-a-war-but-they-still-want-their-own-nuclear-weapons/. More recent polling by the U.S. government similarly shows majority support among South Koreans for an indigenous nuclear weapons capability.

65   Susan J. Koch, "Extended deterrence and the future of the nuclear nonproliferation treaty," *Comparative Strategy* 39, no. 3 (April 2020): pp. 239, 243-244, https://www.tandfonline.com/doi/pdf/10.1080/01495933.2020.1740569?needAccess=true

66   Spurgeon Keeny, "Memorandum for Dr. Kissinger, Subject: Provision of the NPT and Associated Problems," The White House, 24 January 1969, pp. 1, 7, https://2001-2009.state.gov/documents/organization/90727.pdf.

67   Under Abe, the role of Japan's Self Defense Forces was broadened from strict defense of the Japan's home islands to participation in aspects of collective defense, especially with the United States (John Grady, "Panel: Japan's Next Prime Minister Will Continue to Grow Self-Defense Force, Military Ties to U.S.," *USNI News*, United States Naval Institute, 2 September 2020, https://news.usni.org/2020/09/02/panel-japans-next-prime-minister-will-continue-to-grow-self-defense-force-military-ties-with-u-s).

68   Koch, 245.

69 Department of Defence, *2020 Defence Strategic Update*, Australian Government, 2020, section 2.22, p. 27, https://www .defence.gov.au/StrategicUpdate-2020/docs/2020_Defence_Strategic_Update.pdf. For an interesting discussion of the new language, see Rod Lyon, "Defence update signals Australia's waning faith in US extended deterrence," *The Strategist*, 6 July 2020, https://www.aspistrategist.org.au/defence-update-signals-australias-waning-faith-in-us-extended-deterrence/.

70 North Atlantic Treaty Organization, "NATO Secretary General announces increased defense spending by allies," press release, 29 November 2019, https://www.nato.int/cps/en/natohq/news_171458.htm.

71 The full name of the INF treaty is Treaty between the United States of America and the Union of Soviet Socialist Republics on the Elimination of Their Intermediate-Range and Shorter-Range Missiles (https://2009-2017.state. gov/t/avc/trty/102360.htm).

72 The United States and its NATO allies agree that Russia's testing of its 9M729 (SCC-8) ground-launched cruise missile in excess of the ranges permitted by the INF Treaty constituted a material breach of the agreement (North Atlantic Council, *Statement by the North Atlantic Council on the Intermediate-Range Nuclear Forces Treaty*, North Atlantic Treaty Organization, 2 August 2019, https://www.nato.int/cps/en/natohq/official_texts_168164.htm).

73 The Open Skies Treaty is known more formally as the Treaty of Open Skies (https://www.osce.org/files/f/documents/ 1/5/14127.pdf).

74 The United States objected to Russia's selective interpretation of the treaty over the course of years, which included denying overflight of certain parts of Russian territory and bordering areas. A more complete explanation can be found in Bureau of Arms Control, Compliance and Verification, *2020 Adherence to and Compliance with Arms Control, Nonproliferation, and Disarmament Agreements and Commitments*, Washington, DC: U.S. Department of State, April 2020, Part IV, https://www.state.gov/2020-adherence-to-and-compliance-with-arms-control-nonproliferation-and-disarmament-agreements-and-commitments-compliance-report-2/; and Michael R. Pompeo, "On the Treaty on Open Skies," press statement, U.S. Department of State, 21 May 2020, https://www.state.gov/ on-the-treaty-on-open-skies/.

75 The CTBT is more formally known as the Comprehensive Nuclear-Test-Ban Treaty (https://www.ctbto.org/file admin/content/treaty/treaty_text.pdf). The states negotiating the CTBT publicly stated their concurrence that "zero-yield" would be the standard under the CTBT, but the standard was not written into the treaty. In its 2020 Compliance Report, the U.S. Department of State expressed concern that China was not adhering to the zero-yield standard and indicated that Russia demonstrated it had not adhered to it (Bureau of Arms Control, Compliance and Verification, *2020 Adherence to and Compliance with Arms Control, Nonproliferation, and Disarmament Agreements and Commitments*, pp. 49-51, https://www.state.gov/2020-adherence-to-and-compliance-with-arms-control-nonproliferation-and-disarmament-agreements-and-commitments-compliance-report-2/).

76 Resuming nuclear testing reportedly was discussed at a 15 May 2020 meeting of senior U.S. national security officials (John Hudson and Paul Sonner, "Trump administration discussed conducting first U.S. nuclear test in decades," *The Washington Post*, 22 May 2020, https://www.washingtonpost.com/national-security/trump-administration-discussed-conducting-first-us-nuclear-test-in-decades/2020/05/22/a805c904-9c5b-11ea-b60c-3be060a4f8e1_story.html). In apparent reaction to such reports, the U.S. House of Representatives and Senate each included language on nuclear testing in their respective versions of the National Defense Authorization Act for Fiscal Year 2021. The House version (H.R. 6395, section 3121, https://www.congress.gov/bill/116th-congress/ house-bill/6395/text) prohibits the use of any funds available in fiscal year 2021 for nuclear weapons testing. In contrast, the Senate version (S. 4049, sec. 3167, https://www.congress.gov/bill/116th-congress/senate-bill/4049/ text) authorizes $10 million for reducing the time required to execute a nuclear test, if one is necessary. The final version of the 2021 defense authorization bill is not expected to be acted upon by Congress until after the 3 November 2020 elections.

77 The full name of the New START treaty is Treaty between the United States of America and the Russia Federation

on Measures on the Further Reduction and Limitation on Strategic Offensive Arms (https://2009-2017.state.gov/documents/organization/140035.pdf).

78 In 2002, the United States withdrew from another pillar of nuclear arms control, the 1972 Anti-Ballistic Missile (ABM) Treaty, after concluding that the ballistic missile threat had changed and new technological opportunities had emerged to defend against an emerging long-range ballistic missile threat from rogue states.

79 New START entered into force on 5 February 2011, https://www.state.gov/new-start/. Per Article XIV, paragraph 2, the treaty shall remain in force for 10 years and the parties can agree to extend it for not more than five additional years (https://2009-2017.state.gov/documents/organization/140035.pdf).

80 Andrey Ostroukh, "Putin says Russia ready to extend New START nuclear arms treaty," Reuters, 5 December 2019, https://www.reuters.com/article/us-russia-usa-missiles/putin-says-russia-ready-to-extend-new-start-nuclear-arms-treaty-idUSKBN1Y923K.

81 Marshall Billingslea and Tim Morrison, "Special Presidential Envoy Marshall Billingslea on the Future of Nuclear Arms Control," Transcript of Discussion, Hudson Institute, 21 May 2020, https://www.hudson.org/research/16062-transcript-special-presidential-envoy-marshall-billingslea-on-the-future-of-nuclear-arms-control.

82 John Hudson and Isabelle Khurshudyan, "Trump administration and Russia near deal to freeze nuclear warheads, extend New START pact," *The Washington Post*, 20 October 2020, https://www.washingtonpost.com/world/russia-ready-to-freeze-total-number-of-warheads-for-one-year-to-extend-nuclear-pact-with-us/2020/10/20/2c0b06c0-12bc-11eb-a258-614acf2b906d_story.html.

83 In 1972, the United States and Soviet Union signed the Anti-Ballistic Missile (AMB) Treaty and the interim Strategic Arms Limitation Talks (SALT) agreement.

84 The term "next generation arms control" appears in a presentation by the Honorable Christopher Ford, Assistant Secretary for International Security and Nonproliferation and, as of May 2020, also acting as the Under Secretary for Arms Control and International Security at the U.S. Department of State. (Christopher A. Ford, "U.S. Priorities for 'Next-Generation Arms Control,'" *Arms Control and International Security Papers*, U.S. Department of State 1, no. 1 (6 April 2020), https://www.state.gov/wp-content/uploads/2020/04/T-paper-series-1-Arms-Control-2.pdf).

85 In 1991, U.S. President George H.W. Bush and Soviet President Gorbachev each pledged to eliminate most of their nonstrategic nuclear weapons, a set of unilateral but coordinated pledges known as the 1991 Presidential Nuclear Initiatives (PNI). Following the dissolution of the Soviet Union a few months later, new Russian Federation President Yeltsin said he would continue to implement Gorbachev's reductions and elaborated his own. While the United States moved quickly to execute its reductions, Russia moved more slowly, and the status of the nonstrategic weapons on its territory (as opposed to those that had been based in other parts of the Warsaw Pact and Soviet Union) remains uncertain. It is estimated that Russia maintains between 1,000 and 6,000 (the 2018 Nuclear Posture Review refers to up to 2,000) NSNW of various types, as compared to roughly 500, all gravity bombs, reportedly possessed by the United States, of which roughly 200 reportedly are deployed at bases in Europe (Amy F. Woolf, *Nonstrategic Nuclear Weapons*, CRS Report RL32572, Congressional Research Service, pp. 12-14, 26-28, https://crsreports.congress.gov/product/pdf/RL/RL32572). In May 2002, U.S. special envoy for arms control Marshall Billingslea called on Russia to fulfill its PNI commitments (Billingslea and Morrison, p. 43).

86 Of its new strategic systems under development, Russia has acknowledged that the heavy ICBM (SARMAT) and hypersonic glide vehicle (AVANGARD) would be subject to New START rules (if still in force) as deployed, but not its nuclear-propelled intercontinental torpedo (POSEIDON) or its nuclear-propelled cruise missile (BUREVESTNIK), although these last two are unlikely to be deployed, if even successfully developed, before an extended New START treaty expires in 2026. The KHINZAL air-launched ballistic missile may or may not be accountable depending on whether the aircraft from which it is launched is accountable (Billingslea and Morrison, 3; Ford, "U.S. Priorities for 'Next-Generation Arms Control;'" and Andrey Baklitskiy, "Mapping Out an Agenda

for U.S.-Russian Arms Control," in *Major Power Rivalry and Nuclear Risk Reduction*, ed. Brad Roberts (Center for Global Security Research, Lawrence Livermore National Laboratory, May 2020), pp. 8-9, https://cgsr.llnl.gov/content/assets/docs/Major-Power-Rivalry-and-Nuclear-Risk-Reduction.pdf).

87   *Military and Security Developments Involving the People's Republic of China 2020*, Annual Report to Congress, U.S. Office of the Secretary of Defense, 2020, https://www.defense.gov/Newsroom/Releases/Release/Article/2332126/dod-releases-2020-report-on-military-and-security-developments-involving-the-pe/

88   Bureau of Arms Control, Compliance and Verification, *2020 Adherence to and Compliance with Arms Control, Non-proliferation, and Disarmament Agreements and Commitments*.

89   Billingslea and Morrison; and Ford, "U.S. Priorities for 'Next-Generation Arms Control."

90   Billingslea and Morrison, 4. For a directly contrasting view of New START's monitoring and verification provisions, see Rose Goetemoeller, "The New START Verification Regime: How Good Is It?" *Bulletin of the Atomic Scientists*, 21 May 2020, https://carnegieendowment.org/2020/05/21/new-start-verification-regime-how-good-is-it-pub-81877.

91   For example, see "Briefing with Senior State Department Official on the New START," Office of the Spokesman, U.S. Department of State, 9 March 2020 (1736), https://www.state.gov/briefing-with-senior-state-department-official-on-the-new-start/.

92   For example, see "Nuclear transparency 'hypocritical' without mutual trust: Chinese diplomat," *Xinhau*, 23 May 2019, http://www.xinhuanet.com/english/2019-05/23/c_138081140.htm; and Lyle Goldstein, *Meeting China Half-way: How to Defuse the Emerging U.S.-China Rivalry* (Washington, DC: Georgetown University Press, 2015), 352.

93   Regarding Russian concerns about missile defense, see, for example, Baklitskiy, 11. Regarding Russian concerns about conventional prompt global strike, see, for example, Amy F. Woolf, *Conventional Prompt Global Strike and Long-range Ballistic Missiles: Background and Issues*, Congressional Research Service, R41464, p. 37, https://crsreports.congress.gov/product/pdf/R/R41464.

94   Office of the Secretary of Defense, *Missile Defense Review 2019*, p. 31, https://www.defense.gov/Portals/1/Interactive/2018/11-2019-Missile-Defense-Review/The%202019%20MDR_Executive%20Summary.pdf. In May 2020, U.S. special envoy for arms control Marshall Billingslea also said, "The president has publicly stated that he will not permit limitations on US missile defenses. Russia is a sovereign nation and Minister Rybakov has already clearly indicated to me that he is going to raise missile defenses and several other topics. And so, I'm sure we're going to have discussions. I can't stop him from raising these issues and we'll talk. But that said, I would imagine that the Russians would have to make some incredibly impressive offer, I can't even fathom what it might be, for the president to change that position, if that's even possible. So, there will be talks, but I do not foresee limitations" (Billingslea and Morrison, 10).

95   Andrey Baklitskiy, *The Prospects for U.S.-Russian Arms Control*, A Report of the CSIS Russia and Eurasia Program, Center for Strategic and International Studies, June 2020, pp. 16-18, https://www.csis.org/analysis/prospects-us-russian-arms-control; and Office of the Secretary of Defense, *Missile Defense Review 2019*, pp. XI, XVI.

96   Russia and China formally submitted the proposed treaty, entitled "Prevention of the Placement of Weapons in Outer Space, the Threat or Use of Force against Outer Space Objects" (PPWT), to the United Nations in 2008 and updated its definitions in 2014. It would ban the placement in outer space of all weapons, kinetic and non-kinetic. The 1963 Partial Test Ban Treaty and the 1967 Outer Space Treaty only ban nuclear tests and nuclear weapons in outer space, respectively. The 1967 Outer Space Treaty bans all weapons only on celestial bodies, like the Moon. In December 2015, the United Nations General Assembly passed a resolution urging the commencement of negotiations on the PPWT and encouraged states to uphold a 'political commitment not to be the first to place weapons in outer space'" (Todd Harrison, *International Perspectives on Space Weapons*, a Report of the CSIS Aerospace Security Project (Washington, DC: Center for Strategic and International Studies, May 2020), pp. IV-V, 16, https://aerospace.csis.org/international-perspectives-on-space-weapons/).

97   Robert A. Wood, *Statement by Ambassador Robert A. Wood, U.S. Permanent Representative to the Conference on Disarmament at the Conference on Disarmament Plenary Meeting on Agenda Item Three, 'Prevention of an arms race in outer space,'* Geneva, 14 August 2019, U.S. Mission to Geneva, https://geneva.usmission.gov/2019/08/14/statement-by-ambassador-wood-the-threats-posed-by-russia-and-china-to-security-of-the-outer-space-environment/.

98   Woolf, *Nonstrategic Nuclear Weapons*, 2.

99   Dr. Vince Manzo provides a useful examination of U.S. and Russian options if New START expires in his *Nuclear Arms Control without a Treaty? Risks and Options After New START* (Washington, DC: CNA, March 2019), p. 4, https://www.cna.org/research/NAC.

100 Manzo, 2, 28.

101 On 2 October 2020, Russian Deputy Foreign Minister Rybakov said, "'We know pretty well the positions of Beijing, Paris and London. … They are not particularly interested in this. So the second-best option would be that we continue our dialogue on a bilateral basis while the New START accord is extended'" (Michael R. Gordon, "Russia Rejects U.S. Terms for Arms Deal," *Wall Street Journal*, 2 October 2020, p. A7, https://www.wsj.com/articles/russia-rebuffs-trumps-arms-control-proposal-11601557462).

102 Michael R. Gordon, "Russian Negotiator Doubts China Will Joint 3-Way Arms Accord Sought by Trump," *Wall Street Journal*, 9 June 2020, https://www.wsj.com/articles/russian-negotiator-doubts-china-will-join-3-way-arms-accord-sought-by-trump-11591735208; and Steven Pifer, "Russia's shifting views on multilateral nuclear arms control with China," The Brookings Institution, 19 February 2020, https://www.brookings.edu/blog/order-from-chaos/2020/02/19/russias-shifting-views-of-multilateral-nuclear-arms-control-with-china/.

103 Baklitskiy, *Prospects for U.S.-Russian Arms Control*, pp. 6-7.

104 Dmitry Stefanovich, conveying (via Twitter) Russian Deputy Foreign Minister Rybakov's 22 May 2020 remarks at the Gorchakov Fund, https://twitter.com/KomissarWhipla/status/1263776700598542336.

105 In July 2020, a senior Chinese arms control official said, "I can assure you that if the U.S. says that they are ready to come down to the Chinese level, China will be happy to participate the next day. But actually, we know that that's not going to happen" ("China calls US invite to nuclear talks a ploy to derail them," *Associated Press*, 8 July 2020, https://apnews.com/article/21d08a463232b140839345403407fa86). When U.S. special envoy Billingslea welcomed those remarks as indicating flexibility in the Chinese position, the Chinese Embassy in Washington quickly countered, saying China had "no interest" in joining the negotiations (Nichole Gaouette and Jennifer Hansler, "China dismisses US outreach on arms control talks saying it has 'no interest,'" *CNN.com*, 9 July 2020, https://www.cnn.com/2020/07/09/politics/state-china-us-arms-control/index.html).

106 Office of the Secretary of Defense, *Military and Security Developments Involving the People's Republic of China 2020*, ix.

107 Manzo, pp. 92-95.

108 John D. Maurer, "Future Long-Term Scenarios for U.S.-China Missile Controls," Nonproliferation Education Center, 28 April 2020, http://npolicy.org/article.php?aid=1482&rtid=9.

109 Billingslea and Morrison, pp. 9-10.

110 John P. Caves Jr., "Weapons of Mass Destruction: Challenges for the New Administration," WMD Proceedings, Center for the Study of Weapons of Mass Destruction, National Defense University, November 2016, p. 7, https://wmdcenter.ndu.edu/Portals/97/Documents/Publications/Proceedings/CSWMD-Proceedings-Nov16.pdf?ver=2016-11-03-100653-413.

111 Iran's Supreme Leader Ali Khamenei issued a fatwa in August 2005 declaring that the production, stockpiling, and use of nuclear weapons are forbidden under Islam and that the Islamic Republic of Iran shall never acquire these weapons ("Iran's Statement at IAEA Emergency Meeting," *Mers News Agency*, 10 August 2015, available at Federation of American Scientists website, https://fas.org/nuke/guide/iran/nuke/mehr080905.html). He has reiterated that position since, including on 9 October 2019 (Parisa Hafezi, "Iran's Khamenei says building, using nuclear bomb is forbidden

under its religion: TY," Reuters, 9 October 2019, https://www.reuters.com/article/us-iran-nuclear-khamenei/irans-khamenei-says-building-using-nuclear-bomb-is-forbidden-under-its-religion-tv-idUSKBN1WO15H).

112 Paul K. Kerr, *Iran's Nuclear Program: Status*, CRS Reports, RL34544, Congress Research Service, updated 20 December 2019, pp. 58-64, https://crsreports.congress.gov/product/pdf/RL/RL34544/55.

113 National Intelligence Council, *Iran: Nuclear Intentions and Capabilities*, National Intelligence Estimate, November 2007, Office of the Director of National Intelligence, https://www.dni.gov/files/documents/Newsroom/Reports%20and%20Pubs/20071203_release.pdf.

114 Kelsey Davenport, "UN Security Resolutions on Iran," *Fact Sheets and Briefs*, Arms Control Association, last reviewed in August 2017, accessed on 19 June 2020, https://www.armscontrol.org/factsheets/Security-Council-Resolutions-on-Iran. The UNSC adopted a seventh resolution (UNSCR 2231) on 15 July 2015 that reflected the provisions of the JCPOA, and the preceding six resolutions terminated on the JCPOA's Termination Day of 16 January 2016 (Paul K. Kerr, *Iran's Nuclear Program: Tehran's Compliance with International Obligations*, CRS Report R40094, Congressional Research Service, updated 17 April 2020, Summary, https://crsreports.congress.gov/product/pdf/R/R40094).

115 Robert Einhorn and Vann H. Van Diepen, "Constraining Iran's missile capabilities," Brookings Institution, March 2019, https://www.brookings.edu/research/constraining-irans-missile-capabilities/. In 2017, Iranian Supreme Leader Ayatollah Ali Khamenei said that Iran would not develop ballistic missiles with a range in excess of 2,000 kilometers. Kelsey Davenport, "Iran's Leader Sets Missile Range Limit," *Arms Control Today*, December 2017, https://www.armscontrol.org/act/2017-12/news/iran%E2%80%99s-leader-sets-missile-range-limit.

116 "Reactions to the Joint Comprehensive Plan of Action," *Wikipedia*, accessed on 19 June 2020, https://en.wikipedia.org/wiki/Reactions_to_the_Joint_Comprehensive_Plan_of_Action. [Authors' note: while referencing Wikipedia generally is not a good research practice, in this case it is appropriate as the Wikipedia article compiles a large range of documented international reactions to the agreement.] Of particular note, 42 Republican members of the U.S. Senate took the highly unusual step of sending an open letter to Iran's Supreme Leader to make clear that JCPOA was an executive agreement not approved by the U.S. Congress and subject to revocation by the next U.S. president (Tom Cotton (plus 41 other U.S. Senators), *An Open Letter to the Leaders of Islamic Republic of Iran*, United States Senate, 9 March 2015, https://www.cotton.senate.gov/?p=press_release&id=120).

117 The Trump administration's critique of the JCPOA is addressed in The White House, "President Trump Says the Iran Deal is Defective at its Core. A New One Will Require Real Commitments," 11 May 2018, https://www.whitehouse.gov/articles/president-trump-says-iran-deal-defective-core-new-one-will-require-real-commitments/, and Michael Pompeo, *After the Deal: A New Iran Strategy*, remarks made at The Heritage Foundation, 21 May 2018, https://www.heritage.org/defense/event/after-the-deal-new-iran-strategy.

118 Einhorn and Van Diepen.

119 Board of Governors, *Verification and monitoring in the Islamic Republic of Iran in light of United Nations Security Resolution 2231 (2015)*, International Atomic Energy Agency, GOV/2018/21, 24 May 2018, https://www.iaea.org/sites/default/files/18/06/gov2018-24.pdf.

120 "World leaders react to U.S. withdrawal from JCPOA," *Al Jazeera*, 9 May 2018, https://www.aljazeera.com/news/2018/05/world-leaders-react-withdrawal-iranian-nuclear-deal-180508184130931.html.

121 In May 2018, U.S. Secretary of State Michael Pompeo identified 12 requirements Iran would have to meet in a new agreement, among which were permanently and verifiably abandoning enrichment and reprocessing activities; end its proliferation of ballistic missiles and launches of nuclear-capable missile systems; end its support to the Syrian regime, Hizballah Hamas, Houthis, and the Shia militias in Iraq; and end threatening behavior against its neighbors (Pompeo, *After the Deal*).

122 The international arms embargo on Iran expired in October 2020 under the terms of the JCPOA and the 2015 UNSC resolution implementing the JCPOA (UNSC 2231), though the EU embargo continues until 2021.

123 Only the Dominican Republic voted with the United States at the UNSC on 14 August 2020 to extend the arms embargo on Iran. The UN arms embargo expired on 18 October 2020 (Jennifer Hansler and Richard Roth, "UN Security Council rejects US proposal to extend Iran arms embargo," *CNN.com*, 14 August 2020, https://www.cnn.com/2020/08/14/politics/us-un-proposal-iran-conventional-weapons-rejected/index.html). On 25 August 2020, the UNSC president reported that most UNSC members (again, only the Dominican Republic stood with the United States) rejected the United States' assertion that it had the standing under the JCPOA and UNSC 2231, notwithstanding its earlier withdrawal from the JCPOA, to effect a "snap back" of UN sanctions against Iran that had been waived by UNSC 2231 (Edith M. Lederer, "UN council rejects US demand to 'snap back' Iran sanctions," *The Washington Post*, 25 August 2020, https://www.cnn.com/2020/08/14/politics/us-un-proposal-iran-conventional-weapons-rejected/index.html).

124 See, for example, Rick Noack, Armand Emamdjomeh, and Joe Fox, "How U.S. sanctions are paralyzing the Iranian economy," *The Washington Post*, 10 January 2020, https://www.washingtonpost.com/world/2020/01/10/how-us-sanctions-are-paralyzing-iranian-economy/; and Bruce Love, "Companies caught in EU-US sanctions crossfire," *Financial Times*, 29 January 2020, https://www.ft.com/content/97a75318-16a8-11ea-b869-0971bffac109.

125 David Albright, Sarah Burkhard, and Andrea Stricker, *Analysis of IAEA Iran Verification and Monitoring Report*, Institute for Science and International Security, 4 September 2020, p. 1, https://isis-online.org/uploads/isis-reports/documents/Analysis_of_September_2020_IAEA_report_September_4%2C_2020_Final.pdf

126 Rebecca Klar, "Iran threatens to withdraw from nuclear treaty if Europeans bring case to UN," *The Hill*, 20 January 2020, https://thehill.com/policy/international/middle-east-north-africa/479022-iran-door-of-negotiations-on-nuclear-dispute.

127 U.S. presidential candidate Joe Biden stated on 13 September 2020 that, if he won the election, he will return the United States to compliance with the JCPOA if Iran "returns to strict compliance" with the accord and as a "starting point for follow-on negotiations … to strengthen and extend the JCPOA's provision while also addressing other issues of concern" (Joe Biden, "Joe Biden: There's a smarter way to be tough on Iran," *CNN*, 13 September 2020, https://www.cnn.com/2020/09/13/opinions/smarter-way-to-be-tough-on-iran-joe-biden/index.html).

128 Borzou Daragahi, "A series of unusual events in Iran point to sabotage. How will Tehran respond?" Atlantic Council, 10 July 2020, https://www.atlanticcouncil.org/blogs/iransource/a-series-of-unusual-events-in-iran-point-to-sabotage-how-will-tehran-respond/.

129 Kim Zetter, "An Unprecedented Look at Stuxnet, the World's First Digital Weapon," *Wired*, 3 November 2003, reprinted from Kim Zetter, *Counted Down to Zero Day: Stuxnet and the Launch of the World's First Digital Weapon* (Crown Publishers, 2014), https://www.wired.com/2014/11/countdown-to-zero-day-stuxnet/.

130 Ronen Bergman, "When Israel Hatched a Secret Plan to Assassinate Iranian Scientists," *Politico Magazine*, 5 March 2018, https://www.politico.com/magazine/story/2018/03/05/israel-assassination-iranian-scientists-217223.

131 In 2015, Joel Wit and Sun Young Ahn estimated that North Korea had 10-16 nuclear weapons, and projected from 20 to 100 nuclear weapons by 2020 depending on different assumptions, with 50 being the "medium case" scenario (Joel S. Wit and Sun Young Ahn, "North Korea's Nuclear Futures: Technology and Strategy," U.S.-Korea Institute at School of Advanced International Studies, Johns Hopkins University, 2015, p. 7, https://38north.org/wp-content/uploads/2015/02/NKNF-NK-Nuclear-Futures-Wit-0215.pdf). In 2017, David Albright projected 25-60 nuclear weapons by 2020 (David Albright, "North Korea's Nuclear Capabilities: A Fresh Look," briefing, Institute for Science and International Security, 22 April 2017, slide 34, https://isis-online.org/isis-reports/detail/north-koreas-nuclear-capabilities-a-fresh-look-power-point-slides/10).

132 Mary Beth D. Nikitin and Samuel D. Ryder, "North Korea's Nuclear Weapons and Missile Programs," *In Focus*, Congressional Research Service, IF10472, Version 17 – Update, 14 July 2020, https://crsreports.congress.gov/product/pdf/IF/IF10472.

133 Kelsey Davenport and Julia Masterson, *Chronology of U.S.-North Korean Nuclear and Missile Diplomacy*, Arms Control Association, last updated July 2020, https://www.armscontrol.org/factsheets/dprkchron.

134 *Global Nuclear Landscape 2018*, Defense Intelligence Agency, DIA-05-1712-016, 2018, p. 24, https://www.dia.mil/Portals/27/Documents/News/Military%20Power%20Publications/Global_Nuclear_Landscape_2018.pdf.

135 *Report of the Panel of Experts established pursuant to resolution 1874 (2009)*, United Nations Security Council, S/2020/840, 28 August 2020, p. 7, https://undocs.org/S/2020/840.

136 Davenport and Masterson.

137 Kim Tong-Hyung, "North Korea unveils new weapons at military parade," *Associated Press*, 9 October 2020, https://apnews.com/article/seoul-south-korea-north-korea-parades-kim-il-sung-7546d192ecb97af563e797006684bb17.

138 Davenport and Masterson.

139 Shane Smith, "Renewing US Extended Deterrence Commitments Against North Korea, *38 North*, Stimson Center, 13 May 2020, https://www.38north.org/2020/05/ssmith051320/.

140 Lee Haye-ah, "Trump suggests North Korea leader expected war with U.S.," *Yonhap News Agency*, 11 August 2020, https://en.yna.co.kr/view/AEN20200812000300325.

141 *Joint Statement of President Donald J. Trump of the United States of American and Chairman Kim Jong Un of the Democratic People's Republic of Korea at the Singapore Summit*, The White House, 12 June 2018, https://www.whitehouse.gov/briefings-statements/joint-statement-president-donald-j-trump-united-states-america-chairman-kim-jong-un-democratic-peoples-republic-korea-singapore-summit/.

142 Nyshka Chandran, "'Denuclearization likely means different things to Trump and Kim Jong Un," *CNBC*, 12 April 2018, https://www.cnbc.com/2018/04/12/us-and-north-korea-have-different-definitions-of-denuclearization.html.

143 For example, see Victor Cha, and Sue Mi Terry, "Assessment of the Singapore Summit," Center for Strategic and International Studies, 12 June 2018, https://www.csis.org/analysis/assessment-singapore-summit; Michael Green, "North Korea and America's Second Summit: Here Is What Michael Green Thinks Will Happen," *National Interest*, 6 February 2019, https://nationalinterest.org/blog/korea-watch/north-korea-and-america%E2%80%99s-second-summit-here%E2%80%99s-what-michael-green-thinks-will; and Jeongmin Kim and Josh Smith, "North Korean media says denuclearization includes ending 'U.S. nuclear threat,'" Reuters, 20 December 2018, https://www.reuters.com/article/us-northkorea-usa-denuclearisation/north-korea-media-says-denuclearization-includes-ending-u-s-nuclear-threat-idUSKCN1OJ0J1.

144 On 20 April 2018, North Korean leader Kim Jong Un announced that his country "will stop nuclear tests and launches of intercontinental ballistic missiles effective immediately" and would shut down its nuclear test site at Punggye-ri. He explained that North Korea no longer had a need to test nuclear weapons or long-range ballistic missiles, apparently because it had achieved its objectives for these types of systems (Anna Fifield, "North Korea says it will suspend nuclear and missile tests, shut down test site," *The Washington Post*, 20 April 2018, https://www.washingtonpost.com/world/north-korean-leader-suspends-nuclear-and-missile-tests-shuts-down-test-site/2018/04/20/71ff2eea-44e7-11e8-baaf-8b3c5a3da888_story.html). On 31 December 2019, however, Kim Jong Un said North Korea was no longer bound by the moratorium (Choe Sang-Hun, "North Korea Is No Longer Bound by Nuclear Test Moratorium, Kim Says," *The New York Times*, 31 December 2019, https://www.nytimes.com/2019/12/31/world/asia/north-korea-kim-speech.html). The Defense Intelligence Agency and others believe North Korea requires more testing of its long-range ballistic missiles to provide confidence in their performance (*Global Nuclear Landscape 2018*, Defense Intelligence Agency, p. 22, https://dod.defense.gov/portals/1/features/2018/0218_NPR/img/Global_Nuclear_Landscape_2018_Final.pdf.)

145 *Report of the Panel of Experts established pursuant to resolution 1874 (2009)*, United Nations Security Council, 2 March 2020, pp. 4, 71, https://undocs.org/S/2020/151.

146 For example, in January 2020, Kim Jong Un outlined "new policies for furthering increasing" North Korea nuclear capabilities (Choe Hun-Sang, "Pyongyang Vows Expansion of Nuclear Arms Program," *The New York Times*, 12 June 2020, p. A10, https://www.nytimes.com/2020/06/11/world/asia/north-korea-nuclear-trump.html).

147 Matt Spetalnick and Hyonhee Shin, "Pompeo leaves door open to possible U.S.-North Korean summit despite tensions," Reuters, 9 July 2020, https://news.yahoo.com/pompeo-says-u-continuing-establish-145556879.html.

148 The United States' definition of denuclearization on the Korean Peninsula was made clear by U.S. Secretary of State Michael Pompeo during a press conference in Singapore on 11 June 2018: "The ultimate objective we seek from diplomacy with North Korea has not changed. The complete and verifiable and irreversible denuclearization of the Korean peninsula is the only outcome that the United States will accept. Sanctions will remain until North Korea completely and verifiably eliminates its weapons of mass destruction programs" (Michael R. Pompeo, "Press Briefing by Secretary of State Mike Pompeo," Singapore, 11 June 2018, https://www.whitehouse.gov/briefings-statements/press-briefing-secretary-state-mike-pompeo-061118/).

149 See, for example, Sebastian Roblin, "Why India-Pakistan's Nuclear Rivalry Is Deadly Serious," *The National Interest*, 3 March 2020, https://nationalinterest.org/blog/buzz/why-india-pakistans-nuclear-rivalry-deadly-serious-129087; and Daniel R. Coats, *Worldwide Threat Assessment of the US Intelligence Community*, Statement for the Record, Senate Select Committee on Intelligence, 29 January 2019, p. 10, https://www.dni.gov/files/ODNI/documents/2019-ATA-SFR---SSCI.pdf.

150 Jeffrey Gettleman, Hari Kumar, and Sameer Yasir, "China-India Tensions Erupt into a Lethal Brawl," *The New York Times*, 17 June 2020, p. A1, https://www.nytimes.com/2020/06/18/world/asia/india-china-border.html.

151 Hans M. Kristensen and Matt Korda, "India nuclear forces, 2020," *Bulletin of the Atomic Scientists* 76, no. 4 (May 2020): p. 217, https://www.tandfonline.com/doi/pdf/10.1080/00963402.2020.1778378?needAccess=true; and Hans M. Kristensen and Robert S. Norris, "Indian nuclear forces, 2015," *Bulletin of the Atomic Scientists* 71, no. 5 (November 2015), p. 77, https://www.tandfonline.com/doi/pdf/10.1177/0096340215599788?needAccess=true.

152 Kristensen and Korda, "India nuclear forces, 2020," 217.

153 Zachary Keck, "India's Su-30 Jets Are Now Armed with Nuclear BrahMos Cruise Missiles," *The National Interest*, 8 January 2020, https://nationalinterest.org/blog/buzz/indias-su-30-jets-are-now-armed-nuclear-brahmos-cruise-missiles-112016.

154 Hans M. Kristensen, Robert S. Norris, and Julia Diamond, "Pakistani nuclear forces, 2018," *Bulletin of the Atomic Scientists* 74 no. 5 (September 2018), p. 348, https://www.tandfonline.com/doi/pdf/10.1080/00963402.2018.1507796?needAccess=true, and Hans M. Kristensen and Robert S. Norris, "Pakistani nuclear forces, 2015," *Bulletin of the Atomic Scientists* 71, no. 6 (November 2015), p. 59, https://www.tandfonline.com/doi/pdf/10.1177/0096340215611090?needAccess=true.

155 Hans M. Kristensen, Robert S. Norris, and Julia Diamond, "Pakistani nuclear forces, 2018."

156 "Pakistan: Missile," Nuclear Threat Initiative (NTI), updated November 2019, https://www.nti.org/learn/countries/pakistan/delivery-systems/.

157 Hans M. Kristensen, Robert S. Norris, and Julia Diamond, "Pakistani nuclear forces, 2018."

158 Coats, *Worldwide Threat Assessment*, 10.

159 "India: Nuclear," Nuclear Threat Initiative (NTI), updated November 2019, https://www.nti.org/learn/countries/pakistan/nuclear/.

160 See, for example, Abhijnan Rej, "Triangles of Instability: Nuclear Dilemmas and How They Feed into Each Other," *The Diplomat*, 8 September 2020, https://thediplomat.com/2020/09/triangles-of-instability-nuclear-dilemmas-and-how-they-feed-into-each-other/; Sher Bano, "Future Nuclear Developments in South Asia: Implications Upon the Strategic Stability," *South Asia Journal*, 16 June 2020, http://southasiajournal.net/future-nuclear-developments-in-south-asia-implications-upon-the-strategic-stability/; and "Missiles of Pakistan," *Missile Threat*,

CSIS Missile Defense Project, Center for Strategic and international Studies, accessed on 7 October 2020, https://missilethreat.csis.org/country/pakistan/.

161 Lora Saalman, "China's detachment from the South Asian nuclear triangle," *Commentary*, Stockholm International Peace Research Institute, September 2020, https://www.sipri.org/commentary/blog/2020/chinas-detachment-south-asian-nuclear-triangle.

162 Toby Dalton and Tong Zhao, *At a Crossroads? China-India Nuclear Relations After the Border Clash*, Carnegie Endowment for International Peace, August 2020, https://carnegieendowment.org/2020/08/19/at-crossroads-china-india-nuclear-relations-after-border-clash-pub-82489.

163 Office of Disarmament Affairs, "Treaty on the prohibition of nuclear weapons," United Nations, accessed on 29 October 2020, http://disarmament.un.org/treaties/t/tpnw; and "Historic Milestone: UN Treaty on the Prohibition of Nuclear Weapons reaches 50 ratifications needed for entry into force," ICAN, accessed on 29 October 2020, https://www.icanw.org/historic_milestone_un_treaty_on_the_prohibition_of_nuclear_weapons_reaches_50_ratifications_needed_for_entry_into_force.

164 See for example, "Historic Milestone;" and Treasa Dunworth, "The Treaty on the Prohibition of Nuclear Weapons," *American Society of International Law* 21 no. 12 (31 October 2017), https://www.asil.org/insights/volume/21/issue/12/treaty-prohibition-nuclear-weapons#_edn7.

165 New Zealand has signed the TPNW, but the United States suspended its security guarantee to New Zealand under the ANZUS Treaty in 1985 because New Zealand banned nuclear-armed or -powered ships from its ports.

166 The United States holds that the TPNW is ineffective, as it will not result in the elimination of any nuclear weapons because no state that actually possesses such weapons supports the treaty; unrealistic, as it fails to establish the conditions only under which those that possess nuclear weapons would consider giving them up; and counterproductive, as it would delegitimize the essential means of the deterrence relationships that have prevented aggression and dissuaded states from acquiring their own nuclear weapons ("Briefing on Nuclear Ban Treaty by NSC Senior Director Christopher Ford," Carnegie Endowment for International Peace, 22 August 2017, https://carnegieendowment.org/2017/08/22/briefing-on-nuclear-ban-treaty-by-nsc-senior-director-christopher-ford-event-5675).

167 Office of the Spokesman, "United States Hosts the Creating the Environment for Nuclear Disarmament Working Group Kick-off Plenary Meeting, 2 July 2019," U.S. Department of State, https://www.state.gov/united-states-hosts-the-creating-an-environment-for-nuclear-disarmament-working-group-kick-off-plenary-meeting/.

168 Christopher Ashley Ford, "Reframing Disarmament Discourse," Remarks to a virtual meeting of the Creating an Environment for Nuclear Disarmament (CEND), U.S. Department of State, 3 September 2020, https://www.state.gov/reframing-disarmament-discourse/.

169 Wilfred Wan, "Why the 2015 NPT Review Conference Fell Apart," Centre for Policy Research, United Nations University, 28 May 2015, https://cpr.unu.edu/why-the-2015-npt-review-conference-fell-apart.html.

170 The coronavirus pandemic resulted in the 2020 NPT Review Conference being postponed from April-May 2020 to a date to be determined in 2021 ("2020 NPT Review Conference (POSTPONED)," UNHQ, https://www.disarmament.ch/events/2020-npt-revcon/).

171 The full name of the CWC is Convention on the Prohibition of the Development, Production, Stockpiling and Use of Chemical Weapons and on Their Destruction (https://www.opcw.org/chemical-weapons-convention).

172 The full name of the BWC is Convention on the Prohibition of the Development, Production and Stockpiling of Bacteriological (Biological) and Toxin Weapons and on Their Destruction http://disarmament.un.org/treaties/t/bwc/text).

173 A report by the Global Public Policy Institute released in February 2019 concluded that at least 336 chemical weapons attacks occurred over the course of the Syrian civil war, which began in 2011, and around 98 percent of those attacks can be attributed to the Syrian regime (Tobias Schneider and Theresa Lütkefend, *Nowhere to Hide: The Logic*

of Chemical Weapons Use in Syria, Global Public Policy Institute, February 2019, p. 3, https://www.gppi.net/media/GPPi_Schneider_Luetkefend_2019_Nowhere_to_Hide_Web.pdf). A more recent estimate by GPPi of the number of chemical weapons attacks in Syria as of May 2020 raised the number to 349. (https://chemicalweapons.gppi.net/data-portal/).

174 Schneider and Lütkefend, 12.

175 Rebecca K.C. Hersman, Suzanne Claeys, and Cyrus A. Jabbari, *Rigid Structures, Evolving Threat*, Center for Strategic and International Studies, December 2019, p. 11, https://www.csis.org/analysis/rigid-structures-evolving-threat-preventing-proliferation-and-use-chemical-weapons.

176 Hersman, Claeys, and Jabbari, 10.

177 Schneider and Lütkefend, 13.

178 Hersman, Claeys, and Jabbari, 11.

179 Tobias Schneider and Theresa Lutkefend, "The Faint Red Line: How the West Should Respond to the Syria Chemical Weapons Report," The Washington Institute for Near East Policy, 13 April 2020, https://www.washingtoninstitute.org/policy-analysis/view/the-faint-red-line-how-the-west-should-respond-to-the-syria-chemical-weapon.

180 Schneider and Lütkefend, 30.

181 qtd. in Schneider and Lütkefend, 31.

182 James Ball, "Obama issues Syria a 'red line' warning on chemical weapons," *The Washington Post*, 20 August 2012, https://www.washingtonpost.com/world/national-security/obama-issues-syria-red-line-warning-on-chemical-weapons/2012/08/20/ba5d26ec-eaf7-11e1-b811-09036bcb182b_story.html.

183 Office of the Press Secretary, "Remarks by the President in Address to Nation on Syria, The White House, 10 September 2013, https://obamawhitehouse.archives.gov/the-press-office/2013/09/10/remarks-president-address-nation-syria.

184 "Destruction of declared Syrian chemical weapons completed," Organization for the Prohibition of Chemical Weapons, 4 January 2016, www.opcw.org/media-centre/news/2016/01/destruction-declared-syrian-chemical-weapons-completed.

185 Schneider and Lütkefend, 3.

186 Darryl Kimball and Kim Davenport, "Timeline of Syrian Chemical Weapons Activity, 2012-2013," *Arms Control Today*, Arms Control Association, updated May 2020, https://www.armscontrol.org/factsheets/Timeline-of-Syrian-Chemical-Weapons-Activity.

187 For example, see "Syria Sanctions, Department of the Treasury," Syria Sanctions, Archive (2009-2017), U.S. Department of State, accessed on 6 November 2020, https://www.state.gov/syria-sanctions/. In May 2020, the EU most recently extended its restrictive measures against the Assad regime until June 2021 ("Syria: Sanctions against the regime extended by one year," press release, European Council, 28 May 2020, https://www.consilium.europa.eu/en/press/press-releases/2020/05/28/syria-sanctions-against-the-regime-extended-by-one-year/). In June 2020, the United States expanded its economic pressure against the Syrian regime by imposing the first sanctions under the 2019 Caesar Syrian Civilian Protection Act (Office of the Spokesman, Caesar Syria Civilian Protection Act, Fact Sheet, U.S. Department of State, 17 June 2020, https://www.state.gov/caesar-syria-civilian-protection-act/).

188 International diplomatic action on chemical weapons use in Syria has been taken through the OPCW and United Nations Security Council. Russia, China, and Iran belong to the former, and Russia and China also are permanent members of the latter with veto power. They have used their influence in these bodies to shield the Syrian regime from full accountability for its use of chemical weapons.

189 Technical Secretariat, *Third Report of the OPCW Fact-Finding Mission in Syria*, S/1230/2014, 18 December 2014, Organization for the Prohibition of Chemical Weapons, p. 5, https://www.opcw.org/sites/default/files/documents/Fact_Finding_Mission/s-1230-2014_e_.pdf.

190 Distilled from: Technical Secretariat, *Note by the Technical Secretariat, Second Report of the OPCW Fact-Finding Mission in Syria, Key Findings*, S/1212/2014, 10 September 2014, Organization for the Prohibition of Chemical Weapons, https://www.opcw.org/sites/default/files/documents/Fact_Finding_Mission/s-1212-2014_e_.pdf; Technical Secretariat, *Third Report of the OPCW Fact-Finding Mission in Syria*; Technical Secretariat, *Report of the OPCW Fact-Finding Mission in Syria Regarding Alleged Incidents in the Idlib Governorate of the Syrian Arab Republic between 16 March and 20 May 2015*, S/1319/2015, 29 October 2015, Organization for the Prohibition of Chemical Weapons, https://www.opcw.org/sites/default/files/documents/Fact_Finding_Mission/s-1319-2015_e_.pdf; Technical Secretariat, *Report of the OPCW Fact-Finding Mission in Syria Regarding the Incidents Described in Communications from the Deputy Minister for Foreign Affairs and Expatriates and Head of the National Authority of the Syrian Arab Republic*, S/1318/2015/Rev.1, 17 December 2015, Organization for the Prohibition of Chemical Weapons, https://www.opcw.org/sites/default/files/documents/2018/11/s-1318-2015r1%28e%29.pdf); Technical Secretariat, *Report of the OPCW Fact-Finding Mission in Syria Regarding the Incident of 2 August 2016 as Reported in the Note Verbale of the Syrian Arab Republic Number 69 dated 16 August 2016*, S/1444/2016, 21 December 2016, Organization for the Prohibition of Chemical Weapons, https://www.opcw.org/sites/default/files/documents/2018/11/s-1444-2016%28e%29.pdf; Technical Secretariat, *Summary of the Activities Carried Out by the OPCW Fact-Finding Mission in Syria in 2016*, S/1445/2016, 27 December 2016, Organization for the Prohibition of Chemical Weapons, https://www.opcw.org/sites/default/files/documents/2018/11/s-1445-2016_e_.pdf; Technical Secretariat, *Report of the OPCW Fact-Finding Mission in Syria Regarding the Incident of 16 September 2016 as Reported in the Note Verbale of the Syrian Arab Republic Number 113 dated 29 November 2016*, S/1491/2017, 1 May 2017, Organization for the Prohibition of Chemical Weapons, https://www.opcw.org/sites/default/files/documents/Fact_Finding_Mission/s-1491-2017_e_.pdf; Technical Secretariat, *Report of the OPCW Fact-Finding Mission in Syria Regarding an Alleged Incident in Khan Shaykhun, Syrian Arab Republic April 2017*, S/1510/2017, 29 June 2017, Organization for the Prohibition of Chemical Weapons, https://www.opcw.org/sites/default/files/documents/Fact_Finding_Mission/s-1510-2017_e_.pdf; Technical Secretariat, *Report of the OPCW Fact-Finding Mission in Syria Regarding an Alleged Incident in Ltamenah, The Syrian Arab Republic, 30 March 2017*, S/1548/2017, 2 November 2017, Organization for the Prohibition of Chemical Weapons, https://www.opcw.org/sites/default/files/documents/S_series/2017/en/s-1548-2017_e_.pdf; Technical Secretariat, *Report of the OPCW Fact-Finding Mission in Syria Regarding an Alleged Incident in Saraqib, Syrian Arab Republic on 4 February 2018*, S/1626/2018, 15 May 2018, Organization for the Prohibition of Chemical Weapons, https://www.opcw.org/sites/default/files/documents/S_series/2018/en/s-1626-2018_e_.pdf; Technical Secretariat, *Report of the OPCW Fact-Finding Mission in Syria Regarding an Alleged Incidents in Ltamenah, The Syrian Arab Republic 24 and 25 March 2017*, S/1636/2018, 13 June 2018, Organization for the Prohibition of Chemical Weapons, https://www.opcw.org/sites/default/files/documents/S_series/2018/en/s-1636-2018_e_.pdf; Technical Secretariat, *Report of the OPCW Fact-Finding Mission in Syria Regarding the Incidents in Al-Hamadaniyah on 30 October 2016 and in Karm Al-Tarrab on 13 November 2016*, S/1642/2018, 2 July 2018, Organization for the Prohibition of Chemical Weapons, https://www.opcw.org/sites/default/files/documents/S_series/2018/en/s-1642-2018_e_.pdf; and Technical Secretariat, *Report of the OPCW Fact-Finding Mission in Syria Regarding the Incident of Alleged Use of Toxic Chemicals as a Weapon in Douma, Syrian Arab Republic, on 7 April 2018*, S/1731/2019, 1 March 2019, Organization for the Prohibition of Chemical Weapons, https://www.opcw.org/sites/default/files/documents/2019/03/s-1731-2019%28e%29.pdf.

191 Prior to the Syrian chemical attacks, it had been the practice of the OPCW to operate by consensus, at least of the major players, to include Russia. That became untenable as Russia ran interference for Syria at the OPCW as reports of Syrian chemical weapons use mounted, so the organization increasingly resorted to voting.

192 Hersman, Claeys, and Jabbari, 13-14.

193 Technical Secretariat, *First Report by the OPCW Investigation and Identification Team Pursuant to Paragraph 10 of Decision C-SS-4/DEC.3 "Addressing the Threat from Chemical Weapons Use" Ltamenah (Syrian Arab Republic) 24,*

25, and 30 March 2017, Organization for the Prohibition of Chemical Weapons, S/1867/2020, 8 April 2020, p.2, https://www.opcw.org/sites/default/files/documents/2020/04/s-1867-2020%28e%29.pdf.

194 For example, on 9 July 2020, the OPCW's Executive Council adopted, again over Russia's opposition, a decision to condemn Syria's use of chemical weapons in Ltamenah, as attributed in the ITT's First Report (Office of the Spokesperson, "United States Applauds Organization for the Prohibition of Chemical Weapons Condemnation of Syrian Regime Use of Chemical Weapons," U.S. Department of State, 9 July 2020, https://www.state.gov/united-states-applauds-organization-for-the-prohibition-of-chemical-weapons-condemnation-of-syrian-regime-use-of-chemical-weapons/). Further action will be considered by the Conference of States Parties, which may include referral to the United Nations.

195 International Partnership Against Impunity for the Use of Chemical Weapons, website, https://www.noimpunity chemicalweapons.org/-en-.html.

196 Bureau of International Security and Nonproliferation, "About the Proliferation Security Initiative," U.S. Department of State, 19 March 2019, https://www.state.gov/about-the-proliferation-security-initiative/.

197 Technical Secretariat, *Report of the OPCW Fact-Finding Mission in Syria Regarding the Incident of 16 September 2016 as Reported in the Note Verbale of the Syrian Arab Republic Number 113 dated 29 November 2016*, pp. 3-4, https://www.opcw.org/sites/default/files/documents/Fact_Finding_Mission/s-1491-2017_e_.pdf.

198 Technical Secretariat, *Report of the OPCW Fact-Finding Mission in Syria Regarding the Incidents Described in Communications from the Deputy Minister for Foreign Affairs and Expatriates and Head of the National Authority of the Syrian Arab Republic*, p. 4, https://www.opcw.org/sites/default/files/documents/2018/11/s-1318-2015r1%28e%29.pdf; and Technical Secretariat, *Report of the OPCW Fact-Finding Mission in Syria Regarding the Incident of 2 August 2016 as Reported in the Note Verbale of the Syrian Arab Republic Number 69 dated 16 August 2016*, p. 3, https://www.opcw.org/sites/default/files/documents/2018/11/s-1444-2016%28e%29.pdf.

199 For example, in February 2018, Russia and China vetoed a UNSC resolution to impose sanctions on a number of individuals and entities linked to chemical weapons use in Syria ("Russia, China block Security Council action on use of chemical weapons in Syria," *UN News*, United Nations, 28 February 2017, https://news.un.org/en/story/2017/02/552362-russia-china-block-security-council-action-use-chemical-weapons-syria). In April 2018, Russia vetoed and China abstained in the UNSC on the proposal to extend the mandate of the OPCW-UN JIM ("Following Three Draft Texts on Chemical Weapons Attack in Syria, Security Council Fails to Agree on Independent Investigative Mechanism," Meetings Coverage, United Nations Security Council, 10 April 2018, https://www.un.org/press/en/2018/sc13288.doc.htm). In June 2018, Russia, China and Iran joined 21 other countries to vote against the proposal before the Conference of States Parties to establish the ITT; the proposal nonetheless was adopted (Conference of States Parties, "Report of the Fourth Special Session of the Conference of States Parties," C-SS-4/3, Organization for the Prohibition of Chemical Weapons, 27 June 2018, p. 6, https://www.opcw.org/sites/default/files/documents/CSP/C-SS-4/en/css403_e_.pdf).

200 Jack O. Nassetta and Ethan P. Fecht, *All the World is Staged: An Analysis of Social Media Influence Operations against US Counterproliferation Efforts in Syria*, CNS Occasional Paper #37, September 2018, James Martin Center for Nonproliferation Studies, Monterey Institute of International Studies, pp. 1-2, https://www.nonproliferation.org/wp-content/uploads/2018/09/op37-all-the-world-is-staged.pdf.

201 "North Korea used VX nerve agent to kill leader's brother, says US," *BBC*, 7 March 2018, https://www.bbc.com/news/world-asia-43312052.

202 Stefano Costanzi and Gregory D. Koblentz, "Updating the CWC: How We Got Here and What is Next," *Arms Control Today*, April 2020, pp. 16-17, https://www.armscontrol.org/act/2020-04/features/updating-cwc-we-got-here-what-next.

203 Theresa May, "PM Commons statement on National Security and Russia: 26 March 2018," GOV.UK, 26 March 2018, https://www.gov.uk/government/speeches/pm-commons-statement-on-national-security-and-russia-26-march-2018.

204 Steve Morris and Caroline Bannock, "Revealed: anti-nerve agent drug was used for first time in UK to save novichok victim," *The Guardian*, 8 July 2019, https://www.theguardian.com/uk-news/2019/jul/08/revealed-anti-nerve-agent-drug-was-used-for-first-time-in-uk-to-save-novichok-victim.

205 *The Washington Post* counted 46 different story lines that Moscow spun to explain the attack in ways that did not implicate it. While most were preposterous, the Russians sought to create doubt and succeeded. The Russian public overwhelming rejected the notion that their government was involved in the attack (Jody Warrick and Anton Troianovski, "Agents of Doubt," *The Washington Post*, 10 December 2018, https://www.washingtonpost.com/graphics/2018/world/national-security/russian-propaganda-skripal-salisbury/).

206 Julian Borger, Patrick Wintour, and Heather Stewart, "Western allies expel scores of Russian diplomats over Skripal attack," *The Guardian*, 27 March 2018, https://www.theguardian.com/uk-news/2018/mar/26/four-eu-states-set-to-expel-russian-diplomats-over-skripal-attack.

207 Technical Secretariat, *Summary of the Report on Activities Carried Out in Support of a Request for Technical Assistance by the United Kingdom of Great Britain and Northern Ireland (Technical Assistance Visit TAV/02/18)*, S/1612/2018, 12 April 2018, Organization for the Prohibition of Chemical Weapons, https://www.opcw.org/sites/default/files/documents/S_series/2018/en/s-1612-2018_e___1-.pdf.

208 The first set of sanctions, imposed in August 2018, concerned exports of items with potential national security impact (Gardiner Harris, "U.S. to Issue New Sanctions on Russia Over Skripals' Poisoning," *The New York Times*, 8 August 2018, https://www.nytimes.com/2018/08/08/world/europe/sanctions-russia-poisoning-spy-trump-putin.html). The second set of sanctions came in August 2019 and concerned financial and technical assistance as well as export licensing (Morgan Ortagus, "Imposition of a Second Round of Sanctions on Russia under the Chemical and Biological Weapons Control and Warfare Elimination Act," press statement, U.S. Department of State, 2 August 2019, https://www.state.gov/imposition-of-a-second-round-of-sanctions-on-russia-under-the-chemical-and-biological-weapons-control-and-warfare-elimination-act/).

209 Stefano Costanzi and Gregory D. Koblentz, "Updating the CWC: How We Got Here and What is Next," *Arms Control Today*, April 2020, pp. 17-18, https://www.armscontrol.org/act/2020-04/features/updating-cwc-we-got-here-what-next.

210 Robyn Dixon, "Wife of poisoned Russian opposition leader Alexei Navalny blames 'state terrorists' for attack," *The Washington Post*, 3 September 2020, https://www.washingtonpost.com/world/europe/wife-of-poisoned-russian-opposition-leader-alexei-navalny-blames-state-terrorists-for-the-attack-on-him/2020/09/03/c9a375ba-ed51-11ea-bd08-1b10132b458f_story.html.

211 G7, *G7 Foreign Ministers' Statement on the Poisoning of Alexei Navalny*, Media Note, Office of the Spokesperson, U.S. Department of State, 8 September 2020, https://www.state.gov/g7-foreign-ministers-statement-on-the-poisoning-of-alexei-navalny/.

212 The OPCW said that blood and urine samples from Navalny indicated that he had been exposed to a cholinesterase inhibitor (a type of nerve agent) with characteristics similar to, but not among, those novichok agents added to the CWC Schedules of Chemicals in November 2019 ("OPCW Issues Report on Technical Assistance Requested by Germany," *OPCW News*, Organization for the Prohibition of Chemical Weapons, 6 October 2020, https://www.opcw.org/media-centre/news/2020/10/opcw-issues-report-technical-assistance-requested-germany). It was a novichok agent that had not been listed on the Schedules.

213 "Russia's Clandestine Chemical Weapons Programme and the GRU's Unit 29155," *Bellingcat*, 23 October 2020, https://www.bellingcat.com/news/uk-and-europe/2020/10/23/russias-clandestine-chemical-weapons-programme-and-the-grus-unit-21955/.

214 Hersman, Claeys, and Jabbari, 23-24.

215 Michael R. Pompeo, "Report of the OPCW Investigation and Identification Team Regarding Incidents in Ltamenah, the Syrian Arab Republic on 24, 25, and 30 March 2017," press release, U.S. Department of State, 8

April 2020, https://www.state.gov/report-of-the-opcw-investigation-and-identification-team-regarding-incidents-in-ltamenah-the-syrian-arab-republic-on-24-25-and-30-march-2017/.

216 Hersman, Claeys, and Jabbari, 7.

217 President Trump reiterated his view that Russia should rejoin the G7 in 2019 and 2020. Key European allies have objected each time (Amanda Macias, "Trump renews call for Russia to join G-7 group," *CNBC.com*, 20 August 2019, https://www.cnbc.com/2019/08/20/trump-renews-call-for-russia-to-join-g7-group.html; and Quint Forgey, "Trump: It's 'common sense' to invite Putin to J-7," *Politico*, 3 June 2020, https://www.politico.com/news/2020/06/03/trump-invite-putin-to-g7-298432).

218 Hersman, Claeys, and Jabbari, 5.

219 Michael Eisenstadt, *Arming for Peace?: Syria's Elusive Quest for Strategic Parity. Policy Papers* 31. (Washington, DC: Washington Institute for Near East Policy, 1992), pp. x, 31, 51, and 56, https://www.washingtoninstitute.org/media/3641?disposition=inline.

220 Richard Russell, "Iraq's Chemical Weapons Legacy: What Others Might Learn from Saddam," *The Middle East Journal* 59, no. 2 (Spring 2005): pp. 197-199, 203-204, https://www.jstor.org/stable/pdf/4330124.pdf?refreqid=excelsior%3A66a3150828b1d970411cf1398a0e8f95.

221 Gregory D. Koblentz, "Regime Security: A New Theory for Understanding the Proliferation of Chemical and Biological Weapons," *Contemporary Security Policy* 34, no. 3 (November 2013): 501-525, https://www.tandfonline.com/doi/full/10.1080/13523260.2013.842298.

222 If the most capable member of the international opposition (in this case, the United States) also is unwilling to enter new conflicts after prosecuting a decade of war, all the better, but that is a matter of fortuitous timing.

223 For example, see *Global Strategic Trends,* 132-133; *Global Trends: Paradox of Progress,* 21; and *Providing for the Common Defense,* 9.

224 Joseph L. Votel, Charles T. Cleveland, Charles T. Connett, and Will Irvin, "Unconventional Warfare in the Gray Zone," *Joint Forces Quarterly* 80, 1st Quarter (2016), p. 102, https://ndupress.ndu.edu/JFQ/Joint-Force-Quarterly-80/Article/643108/unconventional-warfare-in-the-gray-zone/.

225 Hersman, Claeys, and Jabbari, 7.

226 *Compliance with the Convention on the Prohibitions of the Development, Production, Stockpiling and Use of Chemical Weapons and on Their Destruction,* U.S. Department of State, June 2020, pp. 9, 12, 13, https://www.state.gov/wp-content/uploads/2020/06/2020-10C-Report-Unclassified-Version-for-H.pdf.

227 Caves and Carus, 43-44.

228 Executive Council, *Statement by H.E. Ambassador Heinz Walker-Nederkoorn, Permanent Representative of Switzerland to the OPCW, at the Ninety-Second Session of the Executive Council,* EC-92/NAT.17, 11 October 2019, Organization for the Prohibition of Chemical Weapons, https://www.opcw.org/sites/default/files/documents/2019/10/ec92nat17%28e%29.pdf.

229 Conference of States Parties, *Statement by Andrea Hall, Senior Director for Weapons of Mass Destruction and Counterproliferation, National Security Council, Delegation of the United States of America to the Twenty-Second Session of the Conference of States Parties,* C-22/NAT.7, 27 November 2017, Organization for the Prohibition of Chemical Weapons, p. 1, https://www.opcw.org/sites/default/files/documents/CSP/C-22/national_statements/USA_NAT.pdf.

230 See, for example, Betsy Swan Woodruff, "State report: Russian, Chinese and Iranian disinformation narratives echo one another," *Politico*, 21 April 2020, https://www.politico.com/news/2020/04/21/russia-china-iran-disinformation-coronavirus-state-department-193107; and Edward Wong, Matthew Rosenberg, and Julian E. Barnes, "Chinese Agents Spread Messages That Sowed Virus Panic in U.S., Officials Say," *The New York Times*, 22 April 2020, https://www.nytimes.com/2020/04/22/us/politics/coronavirus-china-disinformation.html.

231 John Hudson and Nate Jones, "State department releases cable that launched claims that coronavirus escaped from Chinese lab," *The Washington Post*, 17 July 2020, https://www.washingtonpost.com/national-security/state-depart ment-releases-cable-that-launched-claims-that-coronavirus-escaped-from-chinese-lab/2020/07/17/63deae58-c861-11ea-a9d3-74640f25b953_story.html; and Tom Cotton, "Coronavirus and the Laboratories in Wuhan," *Wall Street Journal*, 22 April 2020, https://www.wsj.com/articles/coronavirus-and-the-laboratories-in-wuhan-11587486996.

232 Warrick and Troianovski.

233 Regarding how Russian disinformation on the novichok incident played within Russia, see Warrick and Troianovski. Regarding how Chinese disinformation on coronavirus has played within China, see Tanner Brown, "Inside China's campaign to blame the U.S. for the coronavirus pandemic," *MarketWatch*, 15 March 2020, https://www.marketwatch.com/story/inside-chinas-campaign-to-blame-the-us-for-the-coronavirus-pandemic-2020-03-15; and Laura Rosenberger, "China's Coronavirus Information Offensive," *Foreign Affairs*, 22 April 2020, https://www.foreignaffairs.com/articles/china/2020-04-22/chinas-coronavirus-information-offensive.

234 For example, a number of countries who often align with Russia against Western countries in international forums, such as China, Iran, and Bolivia, either voiced support for or abstained from challenging Russia's position when Russia's involvement in the Skripal poisonings was addressed at the OPCW in April 2018 and in the UNSC in September 2018 ("Russian Federation Nationals to Be Charged in Salisbury Chemical Attack, Delegate for United Kingdom Tells Security Council," United Nations, 6 September 2018, https://www.un.org/press/en/2018/sc13488.doc.htm; and "Russia Loses Vote by Chemical-Weapons Watchdog on New U.K. Poisoning Probe," Radio Free Europe and Radio Liberty, 4 April 2018, https://rferl.org/a/russia-skripal-poisoning-opcw-emergency-meeting/29145154.html).

235 As a non-state actor, Islamic State is not a CWC member or even eligible to be one.

236 A significant exception may be the suspected IS chemical attacks in Taza, Iraq in March 2016, where a small number of individuals were killed and some 600 injured. See "Iraqi Officials: IS Chemical Attacks Kill Child, Wound 600," *VOA News*, 12 March 2016, https://www.voanews.com/world-news/middle-east-dont-use/iraqi-officials-chemical-attacks-kill-child-wound-600; and Nafiseh Kohnavard, "Iraqi town Taza 'hit in IS chemical attack' appeals for help," *BBC*, 25 March 2016, https://www.bbc.com/news/world-middle-east-35898990.

237 Columb Strack provides a concise but highly informative review of Islamic State's chemical weapons efforts in Syria and Iraq during this period (Columb Strack, "The Evolution of the Islamic State's Chemical Weapons Efforts," *CTCSentinel* 10 no. 9 (October 2017): pp. 19-23, https://ctc.usma.edu/wp-content/uploads/2017/10/CTC-Sentinel_Vol10Iss9-21.pdf).

238 Department of State, *Adherence to and Compliance with Arms Control, Nonproliferation, and Disarmament Agreements and Commitments* (Washington, DC: Department of State, 2020), pp. 56–62, https://www.state.gov/wp-content/uploads/2019/08/Compliance-Report-2019-August-19-Unclassified-Final.pdf.

239 Dan Lamothe and Carol Morello, "Securing North Korean Nuclear Sites Would Require a Ground Invasion, Pentagon Says," *The Washington Post*, November 4, 2017, https://www.washingtonpost.com/world/national-security/securing-north-korean-nuclear-sites-would-require-a-ground-invasion-pentagon-says/2017/11/04/32d5f6fa-c0cf-11e7-97d9-bdab5a0ab381_story.html.

240 Raymond A. Zilinskas and Philippe Mauger, *Biosecurity in Putin's Russia* (Boulder, CO: Lynne Rienner Publishers, Inc, 2018): 351-356.

241 A discussion of why the United States opposed the BWC Protocol can be found in Jonathan Tucker, "Biological Weapons Convention (BWC) Compliance Protocol," Nuclear Threat Initiative, 1 August 2001, https://www.nti.org/analysis/articles/biological-weapons-convention-bwc/.

242 "Joint NGO Statements to Biological Weapons Convention Meetings of Experts, Geneva, 29 July - 8 August 2019," n.d., https://www.unog.ch/80256EDD006B8954/(httpAssets)/263C1D401CA007F7C1258448003720B1/$file/BWC_2019_MX+Joint+NGO+statement_v+29+July.pdf.

243 Douglas Selvage and Christopher Nehring. "Operation 'Denver': KGB and Stasi Disinformation Regarding AIDS," *Sources and Methods, A Blog of the History and Public Policy Program*, The Wilson Center, July 22, 2019, https://www.wilsoncenter.org/blog-post/operation-denver-kgb-and-stasi-disinformation-regarding-aids.

244 Roger Roffey and Anna-Karin Tunemalm, "Biological Weapons Allegations: A Russian Propaganda Tool to Negatively Implicate the United States," *The Journal of Slavic Military Studies* 30, no. 4 (2017): 521–42.

245 Patrick Tucker, "Iranian, Russian, Chinese Media Push COVID-19 'Bioweapon' Conspiracies," *Defense One*, March 10, 2020, https://www.defenseone.com/technology/2020/03/iran-and-russian-media-push-bioweapon-conspiracies-amid-covid19-outbreak/163669/.

246 Selvage and Nehring.

247 Paul Cruickshank and Don Rassler, "A View from the CT Foxhole: A Virtual Roundtable on COVID-19 and Counterterrorism with Audrey Kurth Cronin, Lieutenant General (Ret) Michael Nagata, Magnus Ranstorp, Ali Soufan, and Juan Zarate," *CTC Sentinel* 13, no. 6 (August 2020): 1–15, https://ctc.usma.edu/a-view-from-the-ct-foxhole-a-virtual-roundtable-on-covid-19-and-counterterrorism-with-audrey-kurth-cronin-lieutenant-general-ret-michael-nagata-magnus-ranstorp-ali-soufan-and-juan-zarate/. The quoted statement was made by Juan Zarate, who was the Deputy National Security Advisor for Combating Terrorism from 2005 to 2009.

248 Michael R. Pompeo, "Syria Sanctions Designations," U.S. Department of State, 20 August 2020, https://www.state.gov/syria-sanctions-designations-2/.

249 David Cohen, "Remarks of Under Secretary for Terrorism and Financial Intelligence David S. Cohen at the Practicing Law Institute's 'Coping with U.S. Export Controls and Sanctions' Seminar, 'The Evolution of U.S. Financial Power,'" Press Center, United States Treasury, 11 December 2014, https://www.treasury.gov/press-center/press-releases/Pages/jl9716.aspx.

250 "Special report: international banking," *The Economist*, 9 May 2020, p. 4, https://www.economist.com/special-report/2020/05/07/geopolitics-and-technology-threaten-americas-financial-dominance.

251 Meredith Rathbone and Brian Egan, "Coping with the US secondary sanctions tsunami," *WorldECR*, 19 December 2017, https://www.steptoe.com/images/content/1/3/v2/138504/SecondarySanctionsTsunami-WorldECR.pdf.

252 Cohen.

253 Cynthia Roberts, "Avoid Allowing Opponents to 'Beat America at its Own Game': Ensuring US Financial and Currency Power," in *Chinese Strategic Intentions: A Deep Dive into China's Worldwide Activities*, a Strategic Multilayer Assessment (SMA) White Paper, NSI, Inc., December 2019, p. 146, https://nsiteam.com/chinese-strategic-intentions-a-deep-dive-into-chinas-worldwide-activities/.

254 "Office of Foreign Assets Control - Sanctions Programs and Information," U.S. Department of the Treasury, https://www.treasury.gov/resource-center/sanctions/Pages/default.aspx.

255 "Terrorism and Financial Intelligence," U.S. Department of the Treasury, accessed on 14 October 2020, https://home.treasury.gov/about/offices/terrorism-and-financial-intelligence.

256 "Who We Are," website of the Financial Action Task Force, accessed on 14 October 2020, https://www.fatf-gafi.org/about/whoweare/.

257 Juan C. Zarate, *Treasury's War: The Unleashing of a New Era of Financial Warfare* (New York: PublicAffairs, 2013), pp. 49-50, 53.

258 Zarate, 214-215.

259 Office of Foreign Assets Control, "Nonproliferation: What You Need to Know about Treasury Restrictions," U.S. Department of the Treasury, 19 September 2012, https://home.treasury.gov/system/files/126/wmd.pdf.

260 Zarate, 215.

261 *2019 Year-End Sanctions Update*, Gibson Dunn, p. 1, https://www.gibsondunn.com/wp-content/uploads/2020/01/2019-year-end-sanctions-update.pdf.

262 Taylor.

263 Section 232 of the Trade Expansion Act of 1962 gives the president authority to impose tariffs on national security grounds if the Department of Commerce investigates and determines there are security concerns (Taylor, Adam).

264 Kathy Gilsinan, "A Boom Time for U.S. Sanctions," *The Atlantic*, May 2019, https://www.theatlantic.com/politics/archive/2019/05/why-united-states-uses-sanctions-so-much/588625/.

265 Gilsinan.

266 "Special report: international banking," 4.

267 "Special report: international banking," 8.

268 "Blocking statute," European Commission, accessed on 22 July 2020, https://ec.europa.eu/info/business-economy-euro/banking-and-finance/international-relations/blocking-statute_en.

269 *2019 Year-End Sanctions Update*, 32.

270 Roberts, 152-153.

271 For example, see Henry M. Paulson Jr., "The Future of the Dollar," *Foreign Affairs*, 19 May 2020, https://www.foreignaffairs.com/articles/2020-05-19/future-dollar; and "Special report: international banking."

272 "Special report: international banking," 8.

273 "Special report: international banking," 8.

274 The IMF decided to include the renminbi in its SDR because it met its two main criteria: 1) it is a currency issued by the top exporting countries in the world, and 2) it was determined to be "free usable," i.e., "widely used to make payments for international transactions and widely traded in the principal exchange markets." ("IMF Adds Chinese Renminbi to Special Drawing Rights Basket," *IMF News*, International Monetary Fund, https://www.imf.org/en/News/Articles/2016/09/29/AM16-NA093016IMF-Adds-Chinese-Renminbi-to-Special-Drawing-Rights-Basket.)

275 "Special report: international banking," 9.

276 "Special report: international banking," pp. 7, 9, and 12.

277 According to *The Economist*, "The world's financial plumbing remains under America's thumb, too. SWIFT's 11,000 members across the world ping each other 30m times daily. Most international transactions they make are ultimately routed through New York by American 'correspondent' banks to CHIPS, a clearing house that settles $1.5trn of payments a day. Visa and Mastercard process two-thirds of card payments globally, according to Nilson Report, a data firm. American banks capture 52% of the world's investment-banking fees." *The Economist* also observed, "Although the organization [SWIFT] is not American, Uncle Sam leans on it to pressure friends and isolate foes. In 2019, when America threatened action if it did not exclude Iranian banks, SWIFT quickly complied" ("Special report: international banking," pp. 4, 10).

278 "Special report: international banking," 11.

279 Charles Lane, "The dollar is still king. But if our institutions keep failing, it won't stay that way," *The Washington Post*, 6 July 2020, https://www.washingtonpost.com/opinions/the-dollar-is-still-king-but-if-our-institutions-keep-failing-it-wont-stay-that-way/2020/07/06/9923f0c0-bf77-11ea-b178-bb7b05b94af1_story.html.

280 Constanze Stelzenmuller, *Hostile Ally: The Trump Challenge and Europe's Inadequate Response*, The Brookings Institute, August 2019, p. 11, https://www.brookings.edu/research/hostile-ally-the-trump-challenge-and-europes-inadequate-response/; and Zarate, 385.

281 *Peering into the Crystal Ball*.

282 Brewer, 23-24.

283 "Special report: international banking," 7; and Paulson, "The Future of the Dollar."

284 The INF Treaty mandated the destruction of ground-launched ballistic and cruise missiles with ranges between 500 and 5,500 kilometers, as well as their launchers and supporting infrastructure. It also prohibited the production or flight-testing of such missiles ("Treaty between the United States of America and the Union of Soviet Socialist

Republics on the Elimination of Their Intermediate-Range and Shorter-Range Missiles," U.S. Department of State, accessed on 2 November 2020, https://2009-2017.state.gov/t/avc/trty/102360.htm).

285 Michael R. Pompeo, "U.S. Withdrawal from INF Treaty on August 2, 2019," press statement, U.S. Department of State, 2 August 2019, https://www.state.gov/u-s-withdrawal-from-the-inf-treaty-on-august-2-2019/

286 For example, in 2007, Russian President Putin said that other states should be persuaded to accept the same constraints imposed on Russia and the United States by the INF Treaty. He also observed in 2016 that the Soviet Union was naive to have agreed to ban ground-launched missiles and allow the United States to retain its air- and sea-launched cruise missiles (Aaron Blake, "Why Putin won't be mad about Trump pulling out of the INF Treaty," *The Washington Post*, 2 February 2019, https://www.washingtonpost.com/politics/2019/02/02/why-putin-wont-be-mad-about-trump-pulling-out-inf-treaty/).

287 "Missiles of the World," CSIS Missile Project, Center for Strategic and International Studies, accessed on 9 September 2020, https://missilethreat.csis.org/missile/; and Office of the Secretary of Defense, *Missile Defense Review 2019*, p. 7.

288 Office of the Secretary of Defense, *Military and Security Developments Involving the People's Republic of China 2020*, p. ii.

289 The U.S. indicated in 2014 that Russia was noncompliant with the INF Treaty for improperly testing what would later be revealed as the 9M729 cruise missile (*Adherence to and Compliance with Arms Control, Nonproliferation, and Disarmament Agreements and Commitments*, U.S. Department of State, July 2014, pp. 8-10, https://2009-2017.state.gov/documents/organization/230108.pdf). The U.S. Defense Department initiated treaty-compliant research and development on INF-range missiles in 2017 (Mark Esper, "Statement from Secretary of Defense Mark T. Esper on the INF Treaty," U.S. Department of Defense, 2 August 2019, https://www.defense.gov/Newsroom/Releases/Release/Article/1924386/statement-from-secretary-of-defense-mark-t-esper-on-the-inf-treaty). The U.S. announced its withdrawal from the INF Treaty on 2 February 2019. In March, the U.S. Department of Defense announced it would test a ground-launched cruise missile in August 2019 and a new intermediate-range ballistic missile in November 2019. The U.S. withdrawal from the INF Treaty was effective on 2 August 2019. The cruise missile test occurred on 18 August 2019, featuring a Tomahawk fired from an MK-41 launcher. The ballistic missile test occurred on 12 December 2019, featuring a prototype of a new type of missile. Both missiles flew in excess of the 500 kilometers limit that had been proscribed by the INF Treaty. (Amy Woolf, "U.S. Withdrawal from the INF Treaty: What's Next?" *In Focus*, Congressional Research Service, updated 2 January 2020, https://crsreports.congress.gov/product/pdf/IF/IF11051.)

290 Woolf, "U.S. Withdrawal from the INF Treaty: What's Next?"

291 Daniel Coats, "Statement on "Russia's Intermediate-Range Nuclear Forces (INF) Treaty Violation," 30 November 2018, https://www.dni.gov/index.php/newsroom/speeches-interviews/item/1923-director-of-national-intelligence-daniel-coats-on-russia-s-inf-treaty-violation.

292 U.S. Secretary of Defense Esper has said that his department will pursue the development of INF-range ground-based missiles as a response to Russia's actions (Esper, "Statement from Secretary of Defense Mark T. Esper on the INF Treaty"), and also that he would like to deploy such missiles to Asia (Tom O'Connor, "China Warns It Will Act if U.S. Deploys New Missiles to Asian Allies," *Newsweek*, 24 June 2020, https://www.newsweek.com/china-act-us-deploy-missile-warns-allies-1513168).

293 The U.S. Marines are considering a ground-launched version of the longstanding sea-launched Tomahawk cruise missile (David Lague, "Special Report: U.S. rearms to nullify China's missile supremacy," Reuters, 6 May 2020, https://www.reuters.com/article/us-usa-china-missiles-specialreport-us/special-report-us-rearms-to-nullify-chinas-missile-supremacy-idUSKBN22I1EQ). In a February 2020 report, the Congressional Budget Office identified near-term, relatively affordable options for U.S. forces to field a long-range, ground-launched missile by adapting

systems already or soon to be in the U.S. military's inventory, including JASSM-ER, Long-Range Anti-Ship Missile (LRASM), and the Standard Missile (SM-6) (Adam Talaber, *Options for Fielding Ground-Launched Long-Range Missiles*, Congressional Budget Office, February 2020, pp. 1, 13, https://www.cbo.gov/publication/56143).

294 See Talaber, p. 15; and Jacob Cohn, Timothy A. Walton, Adam Lemon, and Toshi Yoshihara, *Leveling the Playing Field: Reintroducing U.S. Theater-Range Missiles in a Post-INF World*, Center for Strategic and Budgetary Assessments, 2019, p. 31, https://csbaonline.org/research/publications/leveling-the-playing-field-reintroducing-us-theater-range-missiles-in-a-post-INF-world.

295 Benjamin Schreer, "After the INF: What Will US Indo-Pacific Allies Do?" *The Washington Quarterly* 43, no. 1 (Spring 2020): pp. 150-151, https://www.tandfonline.com/doi/full/10.1080/0163660X.2020.1736885.

296 In August 2019, Australian Prime Minister Scott Morrison said "It's not been asked of us, not being considered, not been put to us. I think I can rule a line under that." In the same timeframe, a ROK Ministry of Defense spokesperson said, "We have not internally reviewed the issue and have no plan to do so." Japan has not directly addressed the issue. Philippines' President Duterte has been outright hostile at times to the United States, so his country is an unlikely base while he remains in power (Franz-Stefan Gady, "Australia, South Korea Say No to Deployment of US INF-Range Missiles on Their Soil," *The Diplomat*, 6 August 2019, https://thediplomat.com/2019/08/australia-south-korea-say-no-to-deployment-of-us-inf-range-missiles-on-their-soil/).

297 See Gady and O'Connor.

298 In August 2019, NATO Secretary General Stoltenberg said that "everything we do will be balanced, coordinated and defensive," while making clear that "we have no intention to deploy new, land-based nuclear missiles in Europe" ("Secretary General: NATO response to INF Treaty demise will be measured and responsible," North Atlantic Treaty Organization, 2 August 2019, https://www.nato.int/cps/en/natohq/news_168177.htm). Earlier that year, Poland Foreign Minister Jacek Czaputowicz had said his country was "against" hosting U.S. ground-launched, intermediate-range missiles, and that any decision to deploy such missiles would be taken by all of the allies (Kingston Reif, "As INF Treaty Falls, New START Teeters," *Arms Control Today*, March 2019, https://www.armscontrol.org/act/2019-03/news/inf-treaty-falls-new-start-teeters).

299 Tom Balmforth and Andrew Osborn, "Russia asks U.S. for missile moratorium as nuclear pact ends," Reuters, 2 August 2019, https://www.reuters.com/article/us-usa-russia-arms-moratorium/russia-asks-u-s-for-missile-moratorium-as-nuclear-pact-ends-idUSKCN1US13M.

300 "Report: Putin Sends NATO Proposal for Moratorium on Missile Deployment to Europe, *Radio Liberty/Radio Free Europe*, 25 September 2019, https://www.rferl.org/a/report-putin-sends-nato-proposal-for-moratorium-on-missile-deployment-to-europe/30182957.html.

301 Michael Peel and Henry Foy, "Nato rejects Russian offer on nuclear missile freeze," *Financial Times*, 26 September 2019, https://www.ft.com/content/008a176a-e05f-11e9-9743-db5a370481bc. A February 2019 article by *Radio Free Europe Radio Liberty* reported 9M729 missile deployments in Shuya (near Moscow), Kapustin Yar, Kamyshlov, and Mozdok (North Ossetia) ("Report: Russia Has Deployed More Medium-Range Cruise Missiles Than Previously Thought," *Radio Free Europe Radio Liberty*, 10 February 2019, https://www.rferl.org/a/report-russia-has-deployed-more-medium-range-cruise-missiles-than-previously-thought/29761868.html).

302 Maria Kiselyova and Michel Rose, "France's Macron denies accepting Putin's missile proposal," Reuters, 28 November 2019, https://www.reuters.com/article/us-usa-russia-missiles-france/frances-macron-denies-accepting-putins-missile-proposal-idUSKBN1Y21E4.

303 In October 2020, in an apparent effort to boost his efforts to keep U.S. ground-launched INF-range missiles out of Europe, Russian President Putin offered to allow inspectors access to Kaliningrad to prove that Russia had not deployed the 9M729 cruise missile there, contingent on the United States and NATO permitting reciprocal access to their sites (Jake Rudnitsky, "Putin Offers NATO Missile Inspections in Bid to Reboot

Treaty," *Bloomberg Government*, 26 October 2020, https://www.bloomberg.com/news/articles/2020-10-26/putin-offers-nato-missile-inspections-in-bid-to-reboot-treaty).

304 The usual upper bound for the speed of systems categorized as hypersonic is Mach 25, at which speed a plasma forms around the vehicle that can affect communications (John T. Watts, Christian Trotti, and Mark J. Massa, *Primer on Hypersonic Weapons in the Indo-Pacific Region*, Scowcroft Center for Strategy and Security, Atlantic Council, August 2020, pp. 4, 7, https://www.atlanticcouncil.org/in-depth-research-reports/report/primer-on-hypersonic-weapons-in-the-indo-pacific-region/).

305 Watts et al., *Primer on Hypersonic Weapons*, 7.

306 NATO Science & Technology Organization, *Science & Technology Trends 2020-2040* (Brussels, Belgium: Office the Chief Scientist, North Atlantic Treaty Organization, March 2020), p. 18, https://www.nato.int/nato_static_fl2014/assets/pdf/2020/4/pdf/190422-ST_Tech_Trends_Report_2020-2040.pdf.

307 Seth Cropsey, "COVID-19 and the Weapons of the Future, *The American Interest*, 9 April 2020, https://www.the-american-interest.com/2020/04/09/covid-19-and-the-weapons-of-the-future/.

308 Dean Wilkening, "Hypersonic Weapons and Strategic Stability," *Surviv*al 61, no. 5 (October-November 2019), p. 141, https://www.iiss.org/publications/survival/2019/survival-global-politics-and-strategy-octobernovember-2019/615-10-wilkening.

309 See, for example, Tony Bertuca, "Hyten says he is pushing for more money to fund Space Sensor Layer," *InsideDefense*, 12 August 2020, https://insidedefense.com/daily-news/hyten-says-he-pushing-new-money-fund-space-sensor-layer; Sandra Erwin, "SpaceX, L3Harris win Space Development Agency contracts to build missile-warning satellites," *Space News*, 5 October 2020, https://spacenews.com/spacex-l3harris-win-space-development-agency-contracts-to-build-missile-warning-satellites/; and Margot Van Loon, Dr. Larry Wortzel, and Dr. Mark B. Schneider, "Defense Technology Program Brief: Hypersonic Weapons," American Foreign Policy Council, no. 18 (May 2019): p. 9, https://www.afpc.org/uploads/documents/Defense_Technology_Briefing_-_Issue_18.pdf.

310 NATO Science & Technology Organization, 19; and Watts et al., *Primer on Hypersonic Weapons*, 6.

311 Wilkening, 130.

312 Ivan Oelrich, "Cool your jets: Some perspective on the hyping of hypersonic weapons," *Bulletin of the Atomic Scientists* 76, no. 1 (January 2020): p. 43, https://www.tandfonline.com/doi/full/10.1080/00963402.2019.1701283.

313 NATO Science & Technology Organization, 90.

314 Woolf, *Conventional Prompt Global Strike*, 47; and Woolf, *Russia's Nuclear Weapons: Doctrine, Forces, and Modernization*, 14.

315 Paul Bernstein and Harrison Menke, "Russia's Hypersonic Weapons," *Georgetown Journal of International Affairs*, 12 December 2019, https://gjia.georgetown.edu/2019/12/12/russias-hypersonic-weapons/.

316 Defense Intelligence Agency, *China Military Power: Modernizing a Force to Fight and Win*, 2019, 91; and Michael Haas and Niklas Masuhr, "U.S.-China Relations and the Specter of Great Power War," in *Strategic Trends 2020: Key Developments in Global Affairs*, edited by Michael Haas and Oliver Thranert (Zurich, Switzerland: Center for Security Studies, 2020), pp. 39, 42, https://css.ethz.ch/en/publications/strategic-trends.html.

317 "DF-17," *Missile Threat*, CSIS Missile Defense Project, Center for Strategic and international Studies, accessed on 29 October 2020, https://missilethreat.csis.org/missile/df-17/.

318 Office of the Secretary of Defense, *Military and Security Developments Involving the People's Republic of China 2020*, p. 56.

319 In March 2018, then U.S. Under Secretary of Defense for Research and Engineering Michael Griffin said, "'I'm sorry for everybody out there who champions some other high priority … But there has to be a first, and hypersonics is my first.… When the Chinese can deploy [a] tactical or regional hypersonic system, they hold at risk our carrier battle groups. They hold our entire surface fleet at risk. They hold at risk our forward-deployed forces and

land-based forces'" (qtd. In Aaron Mehta, "Hypersonics 'highest technical priority' for Pentagon R&D head," *Defense News*, 6 March 2018, https://www.defensenews.com/pentagon/2018/03/06/hypersonics-highest-technical-priority-for-pentagon-rd-head/). See also NATO Science & Technology Organization, 89.

320 Theresa Hitchens and Sydney J. Freedberg, Jr., "DoD Seeks $2.9 billion for Hypersonics in 2021," *BreakingDefense*, 14 April 2020, https://breakingdefense.com/2020/04/exclusive-dod-asks-2-9b-for-hypersonics-in-2021/.

321 Valerie Insinna, "The US Air Force wants to develop a hypersonic cruise missile," *Defense News*, 30 April 2020, https://www.defensenews.com/industry/techwatch/2020/04/30/the-air-force-wants-to-develop-a-hypersonic-cruise-missile/.

322 Sydney J. Freedberg Jr., "Army Sets 2023 Hypersonic Flight Test; Strategic Cannon Advances," *BreakingDefense.com*, 19 March 2019, https://breakingdefense.com/2019/03/army-sets-2023-hypersonic-flight-test-strategic-cannon-advances/.

323 Sebastian Robin, "The Pentagon Plans to Deploy an Arsenal of Hypersonic Weapons In The 2020s," *Forbes*, 30 April 2020, https://www.forbes.com/sites/sebastienroblin/2020/04/30/the-pentagons-plans-to-deploy-an-arsenal-of-hypersonic-weapons-in-the-2020s/#67b9b5c33a5d.

324 NATO Science & Technology Organization, 18; and Watts et al., *Primer on Hypersonic Weapons*, 19-21.

325 Defense Intelligence Agency, *Russia Military Power 2017*, p. 48, https://www.dia.mil/Portals/27/Documents/News/Military%20Power%20Publications/Russia%20Military%20Power%20Report%202017.pdf?ver=2017-06-28-144235-937; and Defense Intelligence Agency, *China Military Power: Modernizing a Force to Fight and Win*, 2019, p. 38, https://www.dia.mil/Portals/27/Documents/News/Military%20Power%20Publications/China_Military_Power_FINAL_5MB_20190103.pdf.

326 Oelrich, 39.

327 For example, see Wilkening, 137.

328 For example, see Watts et al., *Primer on Hypersonic Weapons*, 9; and Bernstein and Menke. For a contrary view, see Dr. Mark B. Schneider, "Moscow's Development of Hypersonic Missiles…and What It Means," in Van Loon et al., "Defense Technology Program Brief: Hypersonic Weapons."

329 For current U.S. declaratory policy on the use of nuclear weapons, see Office of the Secretary of Defense, *Nuclear Posture Review 2018*, pp. 20-21. Per that document, "Significant non-nuclear strategic attacks include, but are not limited to, attacks on the U.S., allied, or partner civilian population or infrastructure, and attacks on U.S. or allied nuclear forces, their command and control, or warning and attack assessment capabilities." Christopher Ford, Assistant Secretary of State for International Security and Nonproliferation, provides an insider's elaboration of the policy in Bureau of Arms Control, Verification, and Compliance, "Strengthening Deterrence and Reducing Nuclear Risks: The Supplemental Low-Yield U.S. Submarine-Launched Warhead," *Arms Control and International Security Papers*, U.S. Department of State 1, no. 4 (24 April 2020): pp. 1-2, https://www.state.gov/wp-content/uploads/2020/04/T-Paper-Series-4-W76.pdf. For Russian declaratory policy, see Vladimir Putin, *Decree of the President of the Russian Federation on the Tenets of Russian Federation National Policy in the Area of Nuclear Deterrence*, no. 355, Kremlin, Moscow, 2 June 2020 (translated into English), https://www.mid.ru/en/foreign_policy/international_safety/disarmament/-/asset_publisher/rp0fiUBmANaH/content/id/4152094.

330 Woolf, *Conventional Prompt Global Strike*, 48.

331 For example, see Defense Intelligence Agency, *China Military Power: Modernizing a Force to Fight and Win*, 2019, 9.

332 Wilkening, pp. 129, 136.

333 "Russia reveals giant nuclear torpedo in state TV 'leak'," *BBC*, 12 November 2015, https://www.bbc.com/news/world-europe-34797252.

334 Vladimir Putin, Presidential Address to the Federal Assembly, 1 March 2018.

335 Thomas Nilson refers to a several megatons warhead (Thomas Nilson, "Russia's 'doomsday drone' prepares for testing," *The Barents Observer*, 26 May 2020, https://thebarentsobserver.com/en/security/2020/05/russia-prepares-testing-doomsday-drone); Amy Woolf to a two-megaton warhead ("U.S. Withdrawal from the INF Treaty: What's Next?" p. 23); and Bill Gertz to a 450 kiloton warhead (Bill Gertz, "Russia covered up explosion of Skyfall nuclear superweapon," *The Washington Times*, 20 October 2019, https://www.washingtontimes.com/news/2019/oct/20/skyfall-nuclear-cruise-missile-explosion-covered-r/).

336 Woolf, "U.S. Withdrawal from the INF Treaty: What's Next?" 23-24.

337 Vladimir Putin, Presidential Address to the Federal Assembly, 1 March 2018.

338 Gertz.

339 Woolf, "U.S. Withdrawal from the INF Treaty: What's Next?" p. 24.

340 Gregg Herken, "Russia's mysterious 'new' nuclear weapons aren't really new," *The Washington Post*, 15 August 2019, https://www.washingtonpost.com/outlook/2019/08/15/russias-mysterious-new-nuclear-weapons-arent-really-new/.

341 For example, see Amy MacKinnon and Lara Seligman, "Is Russia's Doomsday Missile Fake News?" *Foreign Policy*, 22 August 2019, https://foreignpolicy.com/2019/08/22/is-russias-doomsday-missile-fake-news-putin-hypersonic-nuclear-cruise-moscow-kremlin/; David Bond, "Putin's nuclear claims greeted with skepticism," *Financial Times*, 1 March 2018, https://www.ft.com/content/fb14e78c-1d6a-11e8-aaca-4574d7dabfb6; and Billingslea and Morrison, p. 8.

342 Gregory D. Koblentz, "Emerging Technologies and the Future of CBRN Terrorism," *The Washington Quarterly* 43, no. 2 (Summer 2020): p. 178, https://www.tandfonline.com/doi/full/10.1080/0163660X.2020.1770969.

343 Ben Wolfgang, "Arms race underway as rivals defeat drones, deploy technology," *The Washington Times*, 27 October 2020, https://www.washingtontimes.com/news/2020/oct/27/drones-arms-race-under-way-rivals-deploy-cheap-uav/; Nabih Bulos, "A New Weapon Muddies Old War," *Los Angeles Times*, p. A1, 15 October 2020, https://www.pressreader.com/usa/los-angeles-times/20201015; Shwan Mohammed and Maya Gebeily, "Turkey, Iran deploy 'game-changing' drones in north Iraq," *Agence France-Presse*, 1 October 2020, https://news.yahoo.com/turkey-iran-deploy-game-changing-050222160.html; and Tom Kington, "Libya is turning into a battle lab for air warfare," *Defense News*, 6 August 2020, https://www.defensenews.com/smr/nato-air-power/2020/08/06/libya-is-turning-into-a-battle-lab-for-air-warfare/.

344 Secretary-General, *Current developments in science and technology and their potential impact on international security and disarmament efforts*, A/75/221, United Nations General Assembly, 23 July 2020, p. 3, https://normandiepourlapaix.fr/sites/default/files/2020-10/United%20Nations%20Current%20developments%20in%20science%20and%20technology.pdf; and Kelley M. Sayler, *Emerging Military Technologies: Background and Issues for Congress*, CRS Report R46458, Congressional Research Service, 17 July 2020, p. 7, https://crsreports.congress.gov/product/pdf/R/R46458.

345 Koblentz, "Emerging Technologies and the Future of CBRN Terrorism," p. 180.

346 Vincent Boulanin, Lora Saalman, Petr Topychkanov, Fei Su, and Moa Peldán Carlsson, *Artificial Intelligence, Strategic Stability, and Nuclear Risk* (Stockholm: Stockholm International Peace Research Institute, June 2020), pp. 26-27, https://www.sipri.org/news/2019/artificial-intelligence-strategic-stability-and-nuclear-risk-euro-atlantic-perspectives-new-sipri.

347 Zachary Kallenborn, "Are Drone Swarms Weapons of Mass Destruction?" *Future Warfare Series* no. 60 (6 May 2020), United States Air Force Center for Strategic Deterrence Studies, esp. p. 22, https://media.defense.gov/2020/May/19/2002302435/-1/-1/0/CSDS_OUTREACH1417.PDF.

348 Sebastien Roblin, "Why U.S. Patriot missiles failed to stop drones and cruise missiles attacking Saudi oil sites," *NBC News*, 23 September 2019, https://www.nbcnews.com/think/opinion/trump-sending-troops-saudi-arabia-shows-short-range-air-defenses-ncna1057461.

349 John R. Hoehn and Kelley M. Sayler, "Department of Defense Counter-Unmanned Aircraft Systems," *In Focus*, IF11550, Congressional Research Service, updated 29 June 2020, https://crsreports.congress.gov/product/pdf/IF/IF11426.

350 Kallenborn, pp. 2-3.

351 Sayler, *Emerging Military Technologies: Background and Issues for Congress*, pp. 5-6.

352 Kallenborn, esp. p. 2.7

353 Kallenborn, esp. pp. 4, 9.

354 Sayler, *Emerging Military Technologies: Background and Issues for Congress*, pp. 8-10.

355 Esper, Mark, "Secretary of Defense Remarks for DOD Artificial Intelligence Symposium and Exposition," U.S. Department of Defense, 9 September 2020, https://www.defense.gov/Newsroom/Speeches/Speech/Article/2341130/secretary-of-defense-remarks-for-dod-artificial-intelligence-symposium-and-expo/.

356 Philip J. Craiger and Diane Maye Zorri, *Current Trends in Unmanned Aircraft Systems: Implications for U.S. Special Operations Forces*, Joint Special Operations University (JSOU) Press Occasional Paper (MacDill AFB, FL: JSOU Press, September 2019), pp. 1-2, https://commons.erau.edu/publication/1472/.

357 Craiger and Maye Zorri, pp. 14-15.

358 Selcan Hacaoglu, "Turkey's Killer Drone Swarm Poses Syria Air Challenge to Putin," *Bloomberg News*, 1 March 2020, https://www.bloomberg.com/news/articles/2020-03-01/turkey-s-killer-drone-swarm-poses-syria-air-challenge-to-putin; and Secretary-General, *Current developments in science and technology and their potential impact on international security and disarmament efforts*, pp. 2-3.

359 See Directorate for Joint Force Development, Joint Operating Environment 2035, "The Joint Force in a Contested and Disordered World," Joint Chiefs of Staff, 14 July 2016, p. 18, https://www.jcs.mil/Portals/36/Documents/Doctrine/concepts/joe_2035_july16.pdf?ver=2017-12-28-162059-917); *Global Strategic Trends*, 144; Department of Defence, *Future Operating Environment: 2035* (Commonwealth of Australia: 2016), p. 23, https://www.defence.gov.au/VCDF/Forceexploration/_Master/docs/Future-Operating-Environment-2035.pdf; and NATO Science & Technology Organization, 46.

360 Keir A. Lieber and Daryl G. Press, "The New Era of Counterforce: Technological Change and the Future of Nuclear Deterrence," *International Security* 41, no. 4 (Spring 2017), p. 33, https://www.belfercenter.org/publication/new-era-counterforce-technological-change-and-future-nuclear-deterrence.

361 Austin Long and Brendan Rittenhouse Green, "Stalking the Secure Second Strike: Intelligence, Counterforce, and Nuclear Strategy," *Journal of Strategic Studies* 38, nos. 1-2 (2015), p. 61, https://www.tandfonline.com/doi/full/10.1080/01402390.2014.958150.

362 Wilkening, 143.

363 Long and Green observe that the shortcomings of the hunt for Iraqi mobile missiles during the Persian Gulf War should not obscure the advances that the United States made in locating, tracking, and targeting Soviet ICBMs and SSBN submarines during the Cold War since, *inter alia*, the United States had not invested nearly the time and resources studying the Iraqi missile challenge that they had in the Soviet one (Long and Green, pp. 58-64).

364 Lieber and Press, esp. pp. 37 and 46; and Long and Green, esp. pp. 61, 65, and 68.

365 Woolf, *Conventional Prompt Global*, 36.

366 A good explication of the various forms of entanglement can be found in James M. Acton, *Is It a Nuke? Pre-Launch Ambiguity and Inadvertent Escalation* (Washington, DC: Carnegie Endowment for International Peace, 2020), https://carnegieendowment.org/2020/04/09/is-it-nuke-pre-launch-ambiguity-and-inadvertent-escalation-pub-81446.

367 Some experts on Chinese nuclear forces are concerned that China is commingling conventional and nuclear missiles systems under the command of the PLA Rocket Forces, both through co-location while undispersed or, if not so

co-located, through overlapping dispersal areas. While such co-mingling likely originated as a matter of organizational efficiency, they believe that the Chinese may have since discovered that such commingling may enhance deterrence to the extent that it makes the United States more reluctant to strike at conventional systems for fear that it will inadvertently hit nuclear systems and spur unwanted escalation (Tong See Zhao and Li Bin, "The Underappreciated Risks of Entanglement: A Chinese Perspective," in James M. Acton, ed., *Entanglement: Russian and Chinese Perspectives on Non-Nuclear Weapons and Nuclear Risks* (Washington, DC: Carnegie Endowment for International Peace, 2017), p. 68, https://carnegieendowment.org/files/Entanglement_interior_FNL.pdf; and Acton, *Is It a Nuke? Pre-Launch Ambiguity and Inadvertent Escalation*, p. 11).

368 At the PRC's 70th Anniversary military parade, the announcer indicated that the DF-17 would be conventionally armed (Ankit Panda, "Hypersonic Hype: Just How Big of a Deal is China's DF-17 Missile?" *The Diplomat*, 7 October 2019, https://thediplomat.com/2019/10/hypersonic-hype-just-how-big-of-a-deal-is-chinas-df-17-missile/).

369 A robust discussion of the entanglement issues arising from dual-use situational awareness capabilities can be found in Rebecca Hersman, Reja Younis, Bryce Farabaugh, Bethany Goldblum, and Andrew Reddie, *Under the Nuclear Shadow: Situational Awareness Technology and Crisis Decisionmaking*, Center for Strategic and International Studies, March 2020, esp. pp. 33-38, https://www.csis.org/analysis/under-nuclear-shadow-situational-awareness-technology-and-crisis-decisionmaking.

370 Dina Smeltz, Ivo H. Daalder, Karl Friedhoff, Craig Kafure, and Brendan Helm, *Divided We Stand*, The Chicago Council on Global Affairs, 17 September 2020, https://www.thechicagocouncil.org/publication/lcc/divided-we-stand.

371 See, for example, Haas and Masuhr, pp. 46, 50, and Fiona S. Cunningham and M. Taylor Fravel, "Dangerous Confidence? Chinese Views on Nuclear Escalation," *International Security* 44, no. 2 (Fall 2019), pp. 64, 101, and 106-107, https://www.mitpressjournals.org/doi/full/10.1162/isec_a_00359?journalCode=isec&mobileUi=0.

372 The NATO Science & Technology Organization distinguishes between disruptive and emerging (emergent) technologies in the following manner: "Technological development in Data, AI, Autonomy, Space and Hypersonics are seen to be predominately disruptive in nature, as developments in these areas build upon long histories of supporting technological development. As such, significant or revolutionary disruption of military capabilities is either already on-going or will have significant impact over the next 5-10 years. New developments in Quantum, Biotechnology and Materials are assessed as being emergent, requiring significantly more time (10-20 years) before their disruptive natures are fully felt on military capabilities" (NATO Science & Technology Organization, p. vii).

373 Cyber and nanotechnology were discussed in the 2014 paper. That study anticipated that large-scale cyberattacks against critical infrastructure could prove so disruptive and hard to defend against that the United States would be as dependent upon the threat of overwhelming retaliation to deter such attacks as it currently is to deter WMD attacks. The 2014 paper found nanotechnology to be an emerging technology with significance for WMD, mainly for the detection and delivery of chemicals and biologics, whether for malign or protective purposes. The authors consider those earlier conclusions regarding cyber and nanotechnology still to be valid. The 2014 paper also discussed several longstanding nuclear technologies which it anticipated might become more prominent by 2030. Laser isotopic separation is a more efficient way than centrifuges to enrich uranium. Thorium-fueled reactors can produce an alternative fissile material, U_{233}. Neither has yet emerged to the extent anticipated, perhaps because of the continuing retreat of the civilian nuclear power industry in the West since the Fukushima disaster. Efforts to achieve pure fusion for energy purposes, a technological breakthrough that might enable the development of "clean" nuclear weapons by avoiding "dirty" by-products of fission, continue, but fundamental technological barriers remain.

374 Among better sources of information and analysis on the impact of emerging and disruptive technologies on WMD is the "Science and Technology: Exploring the Implications of Advances in S&T" page of the website of the

National Defense University's Center for the Study of Weapons of Mass Destruction (https://wmdcenter.ndu.edu/Science-Tech/).

375 U.S. Department of Defense, *Summary of the 2018 Department of Defense Artificial Intelligence Strategy*, 2018, p. 5, https://media.defense.gov/2019/Feb/12/2002088963/-1/-1/1/SUMMARY-OF-DOD-AI-STRATEGY.PDF.

376 Stephan De Spiegeleire, Matthijs Maas, and Tim Sweijs, *Artificial Intelligence and the Future of Defense* (The Hague, Netherlands: The Hague Centre for Strategic Studies, 2017), p. 13, https://hcss.nl/sites/default/files/files/reports/Artificial%20Intelligence%20and%20the%20Future%20of%20Defense.pdf.

377 Boulanin et al., pp. 7-8. Regarding the dramatic increase in data available, a 2018 UK Ministry of Defence report on global strategic trends observed, "The volume of the world's digital data continues to grow rapidly. There was a tenfold increase between 2010 and 2017, from approximately 1.7 to 18.3 zettabytes (a trillion gigabytes or 10^{21} bytes). By 2025, global data is expected to rise to over 163 zettabytes, and on that trend, there could be over 10,000 times more data in 2050 than there is today" (*Global Strategic Trends*, p. 99).

378 Zachary Davis, "Artificial Intelligence on the Battlefield: Implications for Deterrence and Surprise," *PRISM* 8, no. 2 (4 October 2019), p. 117, https://ndupress.ndu.edu/Media/News/News-Article-View/Article/1979401/artificial-intelligence-on-the-battlefield-implications-for-deterrence-and-surp/.

379 Esper, "Secretary of Defense Remarks for DOD Artificial Intelligence Symposium and Exposition."

380 Website, Joint Artificial Intelligence Center, U.S. Department of Defense, accessed on 14 September 2020, https://dodcio.defense.gov/About-DoD-CIO/Organization/JAIC/.

381 Thomas A. Campbell, *Artificial Intelligence: An Overview of State Initiatives*, FutureGrasp, 2019, p. 26, https://www.researchgate.net/publication/334731776_ARTIFICIAL_INTELLIGENCE_AN_OVERVIEW_OF_STATE_INITIATIVES.

382 Campbell, p. 15. The United States is generally acknowledged as the current leader in AI technology. For example, see Asa Fitch and Stu Woo, "The U.S. vs. China: Who is Winning the Key Technology Battles?" *Wall Street Journal*, 13 April 2020, p. R1, https://www.wsj.com/articles/the-u-s-vs-china-who-is-winning-the-key-technology-battles-11586548597; Boulanin et al., 126.

383 "'Whoever leads in AI will rule the world': Putin to Russian children on Knowledge Day," *RT*, 1 September 2017, https://rt.com/news/401731-ai-rule-world-putin.

384 Nikolai Markotkin, and Elena Chernenko, "Developing Artificial Intelligence in Russia: Objectives and Reality," Carnegie Moscow Center, 5 August 2020, https://carnegie.ru/commentary/82422.

385 Summary of comments by Brigadier General Matt Easley, Director of Army Artificial Intelligence, Army Futures Command, in *AI, Machine Learning, and High-Performance Computing for the Army Multi-Domain Operations: Forum Highlights*, Board on Army Research and Development, 12-13 August 2020, pp. 2-3.

386 Directorate for Joint Force Development, Joint Operating Environment 2035, "The Joint Force in a Contested and Disordered World," p. 17.

387 Boulanin et al., pp. 25-28.

388 Bob Work, "Beyond the Hype: Artificial Intelligence in Naval and Joint Operations," slide presentation at the Naval War College, 25 October 2019, 20th slide.

389 Davis, pp. 120-121.

390 Edward Geist and Andrew J. Lohn, *How Might Artificial Intelligence Affect the Risk of Nuclear War?* Perspectives, The RAND Corporation. (Santa Monica, CA: The Rand Corporation, 2018), p. 9, https://www.rand.org/pubs/perspectives/PE296.html.

391 The International Committee of the Red Cross discusses, *inter alia*, the problem of bias in AI systems (*Artificial intelligence and machine learning in armed conflict: a human-centered approach*, International Committee of the

Red Cross, 6 June 2019, p. 11, https://www.icrc.org/en/document/artificial-intelligence-and-machine-learning-armed-conflict-human-centred-approach).

392 Davis, pp. 121-122.

393 International Committee of the Red Cross, pp. 121-122.

394 C. Todd Lopez, "DoD Adopts 5 Principles of Artificial Intelligence Ethics," U.S. Department of Defense, 25 February 2020, https://www.defense.gov/Explore/News/Article/Article/2094085/dod-adopts-5-principles-of-artificial-intelligence-ethics/. These ethical principles were recommended by the Defense Innovation Board (Defense Innovation Board, *AI Principles: Recommendations on the Ethical Use of Artificial Intelligence by the Department of Defense*, 31 October 2019, p. 13, https://media.defense.gov/2019/Oct/31/2002204459/-1/-1/0/DIB_AI_PRINCIPLES_SUPPORTING_DOCUMENT.PDF).

395 International Committee of the Red Cross, p. 8.

396 U.S. Department of Defense, "DoD Adopts Ethical Principles for Artificial Intelligence," press release, 24 February 2020, https://www.defense.gov/Newsroom/Releases/Release/Article/2091996/dod-adopts-ethical-principles-for-artificial-intelligence/.

397 For example, Secretary Esper has advocated unmanned vessels as a significant part of the future U.S. Navy (David B. Larter and Aaron Mehta, "With DoD's fleet of 2045, the US military's chief signals he's all-in on sea power," *Defense News*, 6 October 2020, https://www.defensenews.com/naval/2020/10/06/with-its-fleet-of-2045-the-us-militarys-chief-signals-hes-all-in-on-sea-power/). The U.S. Navy reportedly plans to buy two large unmanned surface vessels per year over the next five years (David B. Larter, "5 things you should know about the US Navy's plans for autonomous missile boats," *Defense News*, 13 January 2020, https://www.defensenews.com/digital-show-dailies/surface-navy-association/2020/01/13/heres-5-things-you-should-know-about-the-us-navys-plans-for-big-autonomous-missile-boats/). The U.S. Air Force reportedly plans to pair unmanned drones with manned aircraft in future combat missions (Rachel S. Cohen, "Meet the Future Unmanned Force," *Air Force Magazine*, 4 April 2019, https://www.airforcemag.com/meet-the-future-unmanned-force/).

398 Jeff Mason and Susan Heavy, "Trump says he aborted retaliatory strike to spare Iranian lives," Reuters, 19 June 2019, https://www.reuters.com/article/us-mideast-iran-usa/trump-says-he-aborted-retaliatory-strike-to-spare-iranian-lives-idUSKCN1TL07P.

399 Remarks by PLA expert, 2019.

400 Erik Gartzke, "Democracy and Robots: Perils for Popular Rule in the Age of AI," briefing, The Center for Peace and Security Studies, accessed online on 24 September 2020, 10th slide, https://nsiteam.com/social/wp-content/uploads/2020/01/democracy_robots_10192018.pdf.

401 Defense Innovation Board, p. 13.

402 Boulanin et al., pp. 100-109.

403 *Report of the Scientific Advisory Board on Developments in Science and Technology for the Fourth Special Session of the Conference of the States Parties to Review the Operation of the Chemical Weapons Convention*, RC-4/DG.1, Organization for the Prohibition of Chemical Weapons, 30 April 2018, https://www.opcw.org/sites/default/files/documents/CSP/RC-4/en/rc4dg01_e_.pdf.

404 Davis, p. 119.

405 ZD Stephens et al., "Big Data: Astronomical or Genomical?" *PLoS Biology* 13, no. 7 (July 2015), https://doi.org/10.1371/journal.pbio.1002195; P. Carbonell et al., "An automated Design-Build-Test-Learn pipeline for enhanced microbial production of fine chemicals," *Communications Biology* (2018), https://www.nature.com/articles/s42003-018-0076-9; and T Radivojevic et al., "A machine learning Automated Recommendation Tool for synthetic biology," *Nature Communications* (2020), https://doi.org/10.1038/s41467-020-18008-4.

406 Kelsey Lane Warmbrod, James Revill, and Nancy Connell, *Advances in Science and Technology in the Life Sciences and Their Implications for Biosecurity and Arms Control* (Geneva, Switzerland: United Nations Institute for Disarmament Research, 2020), UNIDIR, https://unidir.org/publication/advances-science-and-technology-life-sciences.

407 Christopher A. Voigt, "Synthetic Biology," *ACS Synthetic Biology* 1, no. 1 (January 2012): 1–2, https://doi.org/10.1021/sb300001c.

408 Diane DiEuliis, Andrew D. Ellington, Gigi Kwik Gronvall and Michael J. Imperiale, "Does Biotechnology Pose New Catastrophic Risks" Current Topics in Microbiology and Immunology, 2019; 424: 107-108.

409 Rachel M. West and Gigi Kwik Gronvall. "CRISPR Cautions: Biosecurity Implications of Gene Editing," *Perspectives in Biology and Medicine* 63, no. 1 (2020): 73–92, https://doi.org/10.1353/pbm.2020.0006.

410 "Committee on Safeguarding the Bioeconomy: Finding Strategies for Understanding, Evaluating, and Protecting the Bioeconomy While Sustaining Innovation and Growth," *Safeguarding the Bioeconomy* (Washington, DC: National Academies Press, 2020), https://www.nationalacademies.org/our-work/safeguarding-the-bioeconomy-finding-strategies-for-understanding-evaluating-and-protecting-the-bioeconomy-while-sustaining-innovation-and-growth.

411 Sonia Ben Ouagrham-Gormley and Kathleen M. Vogel, "Gene Drives: The Good, the Bad, and the Hype." *Bulletin of the Atomic Scientists*, October 14, 2016, https://thebulletin.org/gene-drives-good-bad-and-hype10027; and Kelsey Lane Warmbrod, Amanda Kobokovich, Rachel West, Georgia Ray, Marc Trotochaud, and Michael Montague, *Gene Drives: Pursuing Opportunities, Minimizing Risk* (Baltimore, Maryland: Center for Health Security, Johns Hopkins Bloomberg School of Public Health, 2020), https://www.centerforhealthsecurity.org/our-work/publications/gene-drives-pursuing-opportunities-minimizing-risk.

412 Committee on Strategies for Identifying and Addressing Potential Biodefense Vulnerabilities Posed by Synthetic Biology, *Biodefense in the Age of Synthetic Biology* (Washington, DC: The National Academies Press, 2018), https://www.ncbi.nlm.nih.gov/books/NBK535877/.

413 Committee on Strategies for Identifying and Addressing Potential Biodefense Vulnerabilities Posed by Synthetic Biology.

414 Voigt, "Synthetic Biology."

415 Diane DiEuliis and Gigi Kwik Gronvall. "A Holistic Assessment of the Risks and Benefits of the Synthesis of Horsepox Virus." *MSphere* 3, no. 2 (March 7, 2018), https://doi.org/10.1128/mSphere.00074-18; and James Revill and C. Jefferson. "Tacit Knowledge and the Biological Weapons Regime." *Science and Public Policy* (2013), 1–14, https://www.semanticscholar.org/paper/Tacit-knowledge-and-the-biological-weapons-regime-Revill-Jefferson/808c18126dd12e29a3711c606c81270d54dea6ed.

416 Jean Pascal Zanders, "Assessing the Risk of Chemical and Biological Weapons Proliferation to Terrorists." *The Nonproliferation Review* 6, no. 4 (1999): 17–34, https://www.nonproliferation.org/wp-content/uploads/npr/zander64.pdf.

417 President's Council of Advisors on Science and Technology, November 2016, https://obamawhitehouse.archives.gov/sites/default/files/microsites/ostp/PCAST/pcast_biodefense_letter_report_final.pdf.

418 National Academies of Sciences, Engineering, and Medicine 2019, *Domestic Manufacturing Capabilities for Critical DoD Applications: Emerging Needs in Quantum-Enabled Systems: Proceedings of a Workshop* (Washington, DC: The National Academies Press), p. 6, https://www.nap.edu/catalog/25499/domestic-manufacturing-capabilities-for-critical-dod-applications-emerging-needs-in.

419 National Academies of Sciences, Engineering, and Medicine 2019, p. 6.

420 Defense Science Board, *Applications of Quantum Technologies: Executive Summary*, U.S. Office of the Under Secretary of Defense for Research and Engineering, October 2019, p. 1, https://dsb.cto.mil/reports/2010s/DSB_QuantumTechnologies_Executive%20Summary_10.23.2019_SR.pdf.

421 Kelley M. Sayler, *Emerging Military Technologies: Background and Issues for Congress*, p. 21; Tim Bowler, "How quantum sensing is changing the way we see the world," *BBC News*, 8 March 2019, http://bbc.com/news/business-47294704; and Department of Defence, *Future Operating Environment: 2035*, p. 23.

422 National Academies of Sciences, Engineering, and Medicine 2019, p. 60.

423 Martin Giles, "Explainer: what is quantum communication?" *MIT Technology Review*, 14 February 2019, https://www.technologyreview.com/s/612964/what-is-quantum-communications/.

424 See, for example, Defense Science Board, pp. 3-4; and Biercuk, Michael, "Read Before Pontificating on Quantum Technology," *War on the Rocks*, 13 July 2020, https://warontherocks.com/2020/07/read-before-pontificating-on-quantum-technology/.

425 National Academies of Sciences, Engineering, and Medicine 2019, p. 54.

426 Defense Science Board, pp. 3-4.

427 Some banks and other financial institutions already are utilizing quantum communications systems (Giles).

428 Sayler, *Emerging Military Technologies*, pp. 22-23.

429 National Academies of Sciences, Engineering, and Medicine 2019, p. 12.

430 National Academies of Sciences, Engineering, and Medicine 2019.

431 Additivemanufacturing.com, "AM Basics," accessed on 16 December 2016, http://additivemanufacturing.com/basics/.

432 "Additive vs Subtracting Manufacturing," *All3DP*, accessed on 28 September 2020, https://all3dp.com/2/additive-vs-subtractive-manufacturing-simply-explained/.

433 Bruce T. Goodwin, *Additive Manufacturing and Nuclear Security: Calibrating Rewards and Risks*, Center for Global Security Research, Lawrence Livermore National Laboratory, November 2019, p. 10, https://cgsr.llnl.gov/content/assets/docs/OP-Calibrating-Rewards-And-Risks-Goodwin.pdf.

434 Discussion with AM expert supporting the U.S. government, 30 October 2020.

435 NATO Science & Technology Organization, pp. 106, 109.

436 Christopher Daase, Grant Christopher, Ferenc Dalnoki-Veress, Miles Pomper, and Robert Shaw, "WMD Capabilities Enabled by Additive Manufacturing," NDS Report 1908, Negotiation Design and Strategy 2019, Jupiter, FL/Monterey, CA, Executive Summary, https://www.nonproliferation.org/wmd-capabilities-enabled-by-additive-manufacturing/.

437 Secretary-General, *Current developments in science and technology and their potential impact on international security and disarmament efforts*, p. 17.

438 "Using AM is difficult" (Daase et al., "WMD Capabilities Enabled by Additive Manufacturing," p. 19).

439 Daase et al., "WMD Capabilities Enabled by Additive Manufacturing," p. 16.

440 Andrew Conant, "Additive Manufacturing (AM) and WMD Proliferation," in Margaret Kosal, ed., *Disruptive and Game Changing Technologies in Modern Warfare, Development, Use and Proliferation* (Switzerland: Springer Nature, 2020), pp. 63, 65.

441 Daase et al., "WMD Capabilities Enabled by Additive Manufacturing."

442 Goodwin, *Additive Manufacturing and Nuclear Security*, pp. 15-16.

443 Goodwin, *Additive Manufacturing and Nuclear Security*, p. 22.

444 There are commercial firms that advertise their ability to print items using maraging steel, a material used to manufacture centrifuges, including 3D Systems, a firm based in Belgium (https://www.3dsystems.com/materials/laserform-maraging-steeland), and Shining 3D, a firm based in China (https://www.shining3d.com/solutions/ep-m250/). Maraging steel and specialty aluminum used in centrifuge manufacturing also are commercially available in powder form.

445 Goodwin, *Additive Manufacturing and Nuclear Security*, p. 1; and Tristan A. Volpe, "Dual-use distinguishability: How 3D-printing shapes the security dilemma for nuclear programs," *Journal of Security Studies* 42, no. 6 (August 2019): p. 820, https://routledge.altmetric.com/details/65348913/twitter.

446 Goodwin, *Additive Manufacturing and Nuclear Security*, pp. 19-20; and Volpe, "Dual-use distinguishability," p. 820.

447 Hersman, Claeys, and Jabbari, p. 17; and Koblentz, "Emerging Technologies and the Future of CBRN Terrorism," p. 184.

448 Andreas Zaugg, Julien Ducry, and Christophe Curty, "Microreactor Technology in Warfare Agent Chemistry," *Military Medical Science Letters* 82, no. 2 (5 June 2013): p. 67, https://www.mmsl.cz/pdfs/mms/2013/02/03.pdf.

449 Discussion with AM expert supporting the U.S. government.

450 Discussion with AM expert supporting the U.S. government.

451 Kosal, *Disruptive and Game Changing Technologies*, p. 7.

452 National Academy of Sciences, Engineering, and Medicine, *Biodefense in the Age of Synthetic Biology*, p. 91.

453 Conant, "Additive Manufacturing (AM) and WMD Proliferation," 59.

454 Daase et al., "WMD Capabilities Enabled by Additive Manufacturing."

455 Conant, "Additive Manufacturing (AM) and WMD Proliferation," 60.

456 Daase et al., "WMD Capabilities Enabled by Additive Manufacturing," 41.

457 Eric Berger, "Where will the world's first autonomous rocket factory be built? Mississippi," *Arstechnica.com*, 11 June 2019, https://arstechnica.com/science/2019/06/relativity-acquires-a-large-nasa-facility-in-mississippi-to-build-its-rockets/; and "World Class Infrastructure," Relativity Space, accessed on 1 October 2020, https://www.relativity space.com/infrastructure.

458 Conant, "Additive Manufacturing (AM) and WMD Proliferation," 60.

459 Lorne Cook, "US NATO allies still short on defense spending aims," *Associated Press*, 22 October 2020, https://apnews.com/article/estonia-europe-canada-france-gross-domestic-product-d6592c8267efdac36d66651d13347833.

460 Heather Williams, "Asymmetric arms control and strategic stability: Scenarios for limiting hypersonic glide vehicles," *Journal of Strategic Studies* 42, no. 6 (2019): 789-813, https://www.tandfonline.com/doi/full/10.1080/014023 90.2019.1627521.

461 There is not a fatal inconsistency between advocating for holding to account Syria and Russia for their violations of the CWC and suggesting flexibility in how to approach North Korea's and Iran's nuclear programs. Decisions on what costs to impose on those who violate nonproliferation agreements and norms and when to modify or withdraw them always will have be made in a larger context since a state's national security interests are broader than any single issue or incident, even those involving WMD. There are no absolutes in responding, which is why, for example, that most statutory national security penalties have national interest waivers. Responding to violations is an exercise in the art of the possible; the United States must be, and has been, prepared to adjust its response as circumstances change in the service of its larger interests.

462 An opposing view on being more explicit about America's preparedness to go to war with China over Taiwan is provided in Walter Lohman and Frank Jannuzi, "Preserve America's Strategic Autonomy in the Taiwan Strait," *War on the Rocks*, 29 October 2020, https://warontherocks.com/2020/10/preserve-americas-strategic-autonomy-in-the-taiwan-strait/.